JOB AN WITHDRAWN

A Practical Guide for Managers

Michael Pearn and Rajvinder Kandola
are partners in Pearn Kandola Downs,
Occupational Psychologists, of Oxford

JOB ANALYSIS

A Practical Guide for Managers

Michael Pearn and Rajvinder Kandola

Institute of Personnel Management

Phototypeset by Fox Design, Surbiton, Surrey
and printed in Great Britain by
LR Printing Services Ltd, Crawley, West Sussex

British Library Cataloguing in Publication Data

Pearn, Michael
    Job analysis.
    1. Job analysis. Techniques
    I. Title II. Kandola, R. (Rajvinder)
    658.3'06

    ISBN 0-85292-368-6

The authors are grateful to the Civil Aviation Authority for permission to quote from the job analysis study of air-traffic control officers (case study 1) which they carried out while employed by Saville and Holdsworth Limited. They were employed by the same company when they carried out case study 4 and mini case study 1.

Contents

page 129

1
Introducing Job, Task and Role Analysis

What is Job, Task and Role Analysis?

Almost all managers during their careers will be involved in some
form of systematic data collection in order to solve a problem,
resolve a dilemma, or bring about some change in their organizations. In addition to these more formal studies managers
invariably have to obtain information of one kind or another to
help them do their jobs. Job, task and role (JTR) analysis is a
specific aspect of the manager's job and is defined as: 'any
systematic procedure for obtaining detailed and objective information about a job, task or role that will be performed or is
currently being performed'.

Typically, the analysis is designed to achieve a specific goal and
is primarily in terms of exactly what is done and how it is done,
but increasingly the context or 'culture' is also very important. In
practice, this goal can range from improving the efficiency of
selection decisions to investigating the reasons why, despite the
introduction of new high-speed equipment, production still falls
below the projected targets. In this sense, JTR analysis can be seen
as a form of research. The researcher has a problem to be solved or
a need to be met and information is gathered in a way which is as
systematic, reliable and accurate as possible. In the light of the
information obtained, the problem can be resolved or at least
redefined. Basic skills, as described in this book for conducting
JTR analysis, are crucial to the effective line manager, but are even
more important to the personnel specialist whose function is
often to resolve problems, and to bring about change within an
organization in terms of its human resources.

The term JTR analysis has been used deliberately in this book
to distinguish the subject-matter from traditional notions of job
analysis. For many people, job analysis is a rather narrow and
limited procedure with only specialized application. At one
extreme it conjures up the picture of white-coated men (very
rarely women) with a clipboard and a stop watch observing
operatives. Whereas time and motion has an important role to
play to meet specific needs, it is only one small facet of the

1

ever-growing range of techniques and methods available to managers for the systematic accumulation of data about jobs, tasks and roles.

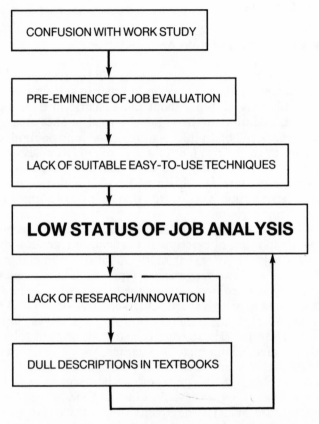

Figure 1.1 *The self-perpetuating image of job analysis as dull and uninteresting*

Until recently job analysis was a neglected field. There was little research and accordingly little innovation and development. To many people it was a dull and uninteresting field. However, during the 1970s and '80s in the United States, the Equal Opportunities legislation, among other things, stimulated a renewed interest in job analysis, bringing about a flurry of research and

2

innovation which has produced a range of flexible techniques which can be used by managers. Also, in the United Kingdom in recent years, there has been a renewed interest which has brought about a parallel development of new techniques. In this book, the authors review the wide choice of techniques currently available so that managers can decide for themselves which methods they wish to use.

Why is JTR analysis necessary?

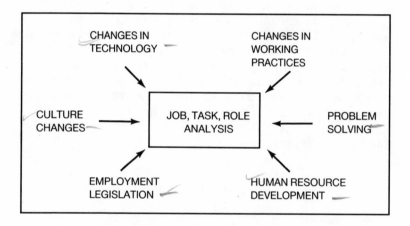

Figure 1.2 *Six main factors contributing to the increased importance of JTR analysis*

JTR analysis is important because, in general, it is better to solve problems on the basis of data and evidence rather than on speculation or by reliance solely on things that have worked in the past. For example, in a cigarette factory the management believed that the newly created post of machine minder combined with mechanic could only be filled by a machine mechanic. However, the JTR study revealed that the job could also be performed by the better machine minders. Many of the things that the mechanics had been trained to do, they never did in practice – whereas, in contrast, the better minders, who saw their job as keeping the machines running, were in fact using most of the skills

3

required in the new minder/mechanic's role. Accordingly the training gap between minder and mechanic was much smaller than had been envisaged.

A brewery conducted a JTR analysis of what made a good publican. For many years, the brewery had recruited confident-looking, outgoing couples to run the pubs, and yet the analysis showed that personality had little to do with determining the success or otherwise of the pub. The study revealed that business acumen, coupled with certain features of the working relationship between the husband and wife, was far more important than the couple's extraversion and social confidence.

JTR analysis can play a significant role in enabling businesses to gain an insight into issues and to define problems. A JTR study carried out by the authors into the underlying causes of the high incidence of vehicle damage and accidents in a transport organization revealed that it was less a matter of the initial selection and training of personnel, as the management had supposed, and more to do with the delegation of work, the role of the supervisors, and the culture that had developed, unrestrained, over a long period, in which vehicle damage was not only tolerated but almost expected.

	RESEARCH	JTR ANALYSIS
Based on data-gathering	YES	YES
Interpretation required	YES	YES
Systematic in approach	YES	YES
Task hypothesis	FREQUENTLY	FREQUENTLY
Can be exploratory	YES	YES
Quantified	WHEREVER POSSIBLE	WHEREVER POSSIBLE
Generalizable	FREQUENTLY	OCCASIONALLY
Generates theories	FREQUENTLY	RARELY
Written up as PhD thesis	FREQUENTLY	RARELY
Stimulus	THEORIES, PROBLEMS	PROBLEMS/ NEED FOR CHANGE

Job, task, role analysis is therefore a form of applied research.

Figure 1.3 *Comparison of research and JTR analysis*

4

With the increasing introduction of technology, frequently associated with changes in working practices and the culture of an organization, there is a growing need for JTR analysis to determine how jobs should be grouped, roles changed, and which forms of job behaviour are consistent with the new culture the organization is trying to create. In a chemical plant where a new manufacturing process operated solely by two people was to be brought in, a JTR study was carried out in order to define the necessary skill level required of the operators. As the jobs did not yet exist, partly because the plant had not been constructed and the computer-integrated manufacturing software had not been finalized, an analysis was conducted of the operators' role at four possible skill levels. Instead of speculating in general, the organization was able to decide which categories and levels of job and task performance would be feasible in the new plant, bearing in mind the people from whom the new technicians would be selected.

Another important function of JTR analysis in new and changing technology is to evaluate the increased demand on operatives in terms of conceptual rather than manual skills, i.e. increased flexibility, greater accountability and continuing self-development. JTR analysis has also been extensively employed to identify underlying attributes and core requirement such as the need for autonomy, readiness to learn, teamworking, flexibility, etc., which can be used for selection, training, and development purposes.

The importance of JTR analysis in human resource development generally has been long recognized. Anyone who has been involved in designing and running assessment centres will know from hard experience that the more specific and concrete the assessment criteria are (based on a thorough analysis), the better the assessment centre will work. Equally it is easier to design realistic tasks which simulate critical aspects of a job if these are based on a detailed analysis. Similarly, the definition of selection and promotion criteria and job behaviour for appraisal and performance assessment will be more accurate and less amenable to bias and distortion if closely based on behaviour that has been studied in jobs.

Identifying training and learning needs are well-established applications of JTR analysis. A study with the Job Learning Analysis of key brewery operatives revealed that the job was being taught in a very mechanistic way, whereby the operators were expected to memorize complex routes of fluids through pipes

5

around the site. In the past the job had taken a very long time to learn, mainly through trial and error, but the JLA revealed that operatives needed not only to memorize this information but also to develop the skills of planning the most efficient routes and to learn from the experience of prioritizing and anticipating the flows of fluids. Therefore the analysis revealed other learning skills which needed to be developed in order for the operatives to work more effectively.

One reason why job analysis is often considered too narrow is that many of the jobs requiring analysis may not yet exist. This is partly because people frequently need to be recruited for new jobs or to assume new roles before the organization has defined the demands that are going to be made on the prospective jobholders. The traditional approach to job analysis has tended to be one of breaking jobs down into a discrete set of tasks and relating these to a specific set of aptitudes or behaviour patterns which need to be acquired or developed. Although there are occasions when a task analytical approach is exactly what is required, this is generally too rigid and inflexible. JTR analysis is a wider concept recognizing that while jobs *can* be defined by a specific set of tasks and/or responsibilities, they can also be defined as roles, i.e. in terms of what needs to be achieved (or job objectives). An example of this might be the bank manager whose job at one level has not changed a great deal, but whose role in selling the services of the bank in an energetic way, in competition with other organizations, may have altered considerably.

Many applications of JTR analysis involve defining jobs by reference to specific tasks or groups of tasks that have to be performed. For example, in an oil refinery a Technician Grade 3 operative must be able to perform any 10 of 20 tasks, a technician Grade 4 should be able to do 16, and Grade 5 should be able to perform all 20. Clearly there is a need for a flexible approach to the analysis of jobs, tasks and roles, one that can be adapted to the varying demands of different situations.

Employment legislation is another reason for the increased and growing importance of JTR analysis. Although there is no legislation in Britain which requires employers to treat all people fairly at work, the current legislation (under the Race Relations Act 1976 and the Sex Discrimination Act 1975, 1986) does protect job applicants and employees from unfair treatment or disadvantage because of their race or sex. An employer may be required to justify a short-listing procedure, or the way in which they conducted an interview, or the criteria used for selection and/or promotion. If an employer is challenged on these grounds it may be necessary to show that the selection criteria or test being used is justifiable. The best way to do this, other than by persuasive argument, is by systematic evidence derived from JTR analysis. Under the Equal Pay Act 1970 (as amended 1983), employees are entitled to claim equal pay for work of equal value and can challenge a job evaluation scheme as biased if they feel it works to the disadvantage of one sex. There may well be an increasing demand by employers for more empirically or statistically based evidence to support the pay and grading structure in operation. Although job evaluation lies outside the scope of this book, some of the techniques described in detail in Chapters 4 and 5 will be relevant to ascertaining whether or not disparate jobs make similar demands on employees in terms of effort, skill and decision-making requirements.

Overview of the book

This book is designed to reveal to busy managers the wide range of techniques (some simple, some highly sophisticated) available to help gather systematic data or information which is relevant to a specific purpose or problem with which they have to deal. Chapter 2 provides an overview of the methods and presents a framework for evaluating their usefulness. A set of criteria are presented to help the manager select a technique for a specific purpose. Chapter 3 systematically describes and evaluates ten of the most useful JTR techniques. Each technique is considered according to the following:

Description This section names the technique and provides a brief outline of how it works in practice.

Applications The main uses of the technique with examples of the kinds of data that are generated.

Limitations This section describes weaknesses, limitations, and applications for which the technique might not be suitable.

Evaluation A summary of the key points for and against the technique.

Chapter 4 contains briefer descriptions of eight other techniques, while Chapter 5 presents five case studies of JTR analyses, all of which were carried out by the authors, which illustrate the process from designing the study, gathering the data, interpreting the results, and implementing the findings; four mini case studies follow in Chapter 6, also based on work carried out by the authors.

Chapter 7 presents a simple, but none-the-less rigorous approach to JTR analysis which will meet many of the needs of managers. Finally, Chapter 8 sums up the state of the art at present, and then looks ahead, identifying gaps in the range of available JTR techniques, which will need to be filled to meet future needs.

2
Choosing a Method

Challenges in conducting a JTR study

In this chapter a framework is presented to help the manager choose appropriate data-gathering methods for a JTR analysis.

One of the main challenges is to conduct a JTR study in a way that does not artificially distort the job, task or role being analysed. There is a risk that when the job or task is broken down into specific sub-tasks or elements, the dynamic properties of the job or task are missed. By concentrating on the microscopic detail, the analyst could fail to see aspects of the overall picture which are critical to overall success. For example, the same set of tasks could be carried out by two individuals; one might proceed with a general level of understanding of what is going on, enabling him or her to show good anticipation and thereby take appropriate preventative action, whereas the other might carry out the duties with little real comprehension and hence poor anticipation. It may be that a certain level of understanding and associated anticipatory skills are critical to successful performance of the job.

The challenge of obtaining accurate, representative, and meaningful data is made more difficult by three factors:

(1) *Time-determined changes* The job is not static but is changing over a period of time, albeit very slowly. There is a very real risk that the JTR analysis in effect takes a snapshot picture which freezes the job, task or role at some specific point, giving little insight into how the job has evolved or will unfold in the future.

(2) *Person-determined changes* The job, task or role takes on different properties depending on who happens to be doing it; thus, the same job could be done with considerable flexibility and responsiveness, or rigidly and mechanistically. This may have more to do with the perception of the jobholder and the context or climate in which the job is done than with individual skills and abilities.

(3) *Situation-determined changes* The job of a firefighter in an inner-city area, although described as identical to a

firefighter in a rural area, would in fact be substantially different in practice.

Eight features of JTR analysis

When choosing appropriate data-gathering methods for a JTR study, eight broad distinctions are relevant. They are:

(1) *Orientation:*   worker or task-orientated methods;
(2) *Quantification:*   quantified or qualitative methods;
(3) *Structure:*   open-ended or closed methods;
(4) *Packaging:*   packaged systems or do-it-yourself;
(5) *Sophistication:*   sophisticated or straightforward techniques;
(6) *Proximity to jobs:*   remote from or close to the job under study;
(7) *Applicability:*   wide application or narrow; and
(8) *Sensitivity:*   adaptable or inflexible.

1   *Orientation*   most JTR techniques can be divided into broadly worker-orientated or task-orientated. Task-orientated approaches tend to focus on the precise activities or tasks carried out by the job incumbent, and the best-known technique is Hierarchical Task Analysis (see Chapter 3). Such methods tend to be used for producing job descriptions, developing training curricula, instigating job performance appraisal standards, and for job design and equipment design. By contrast, behaviour or worker-orientated methods concentrate on underlying skills, aptitudes, and other attributes of people. The main applications of worker-orientated methods are, for example, defining selection criteria, assessment centre standards, identifying and analysing skill needs, grouping jobs, and identifying career development paths.

2   *Quantification*   some JTR techniques produce numerical or quantitative data whereas others produce qualitative or subjective data. In the middle of the range are a number of techniques which produce qualitative data but which can subsequently be quantified. Systems based on rating scales, such as the Position Analysis Questionnaire (see Chapter 3), are at the extreme of the quantification scale and, generally speaking, sophisticated computer programs are required to analyse the data produced. At the other end of the spectrum are methods where a job incumbent is required to keep a diary or a log to describe the activities he or

10

she has been carrying out in a specified period. Observation techniques, including having an analyst sit alongside or near the worker, and the use of video recordings, are qualitative in nature. However, by using an appropriate structure and framework the information can be quantified in terms of frequency and time spent doing particular activities.

3 *Structure* the traditional job-analysis interview where the job analyst goes along to interview job incumbents with a structured but open-ended interview plan is probably the most common form of data-gathering. The level of detail recorded, its thoroughness and the specific things focused on will be very much decided by the interviewer rather than structured by the data-gathering method itself. At the other extreme is the Job Specific Checklist. Sometimes these checklists are developed specifically inside an organization, but there are a number of examples of industry-wide checklists in which several hundred particular statements of job behaviour are presented, e.g. in production engineering, and it is simply a matter of recording which specific tasks the person being interviewed carries out. The advantages gained from the high degree of rigour and thoroughness could be outweighed by the need for responsive flexibility which the checklist approach does not permit, but which is of course a strength of the job-analysis interview.

4 *Packaging* there are an increasing number of packaged JTR analysis systems available. This is particularly the case in the United States where the Equal Employment Opportunities legislation has required employers to justify their selection procedures wherever there is an adverse impact on one sex or on a minority group. As a result, a flurry of packaged job-analysis techniques appeared on the American market in the 1970s and '80s. The systems frequently cover the whole process from formulating objectives to interpreting and presenting the results. Invariably, they are computer-assisted. An example of a British packaged system, but one which does not require computer analysis, is the Job Components Inventory (described in Chapter 3). At the opposite end of the spectrum is the do-it-yourself approach, e.g. an internally developed checklist, rating scale or structured-interview plan. These can be effective in meeting the managers' needs, especially if rules are laid down for determining what constitutes suitable evidence. There are clear advantages in terms of cheapness and ability to gear the data-gathering to the

11

organization's own needs rather than bend them to fit into a general system. On the other hand, the general systems frequently have greater statistical power, giving greater reliability to the results.

5 *Sophisitication* a number of techniques that are currently available require a relatively high level of knowledge and understanding on the part of the user. The more sophisticated methods may make greater demands in terms of the time involved, understanding of statistics, and the complexity of the process required to operate the whole system. A fully fledged PAQ (Position Analysis Questionnaire) study will result in computer printouts showing standard errors of measurement, cluster analysis, and reliability co-efficients. Whereas this is not beyond the reach of many personnel managers (particularly those who are trained, for example, in the use of personality questionnaires), it may inhibit others from using a technique. At the other end of the spectrum there are a large number of techniques available which can easily be used. These include diaries or logs, observation, checklists (such as the Trainer Task Inventory) and structured interviews.

6 *Proximity to jobs* JTR data-gathering methods vary in their closeness to the job, task or role under study. At one extreme, participant observation actually involves performing the job itself, or undergoing the training. Although time-consuming, it can produce insights which cannot be gained in any other way. Other techniques which are relatively close to the job and do not influence or distort what is being studied include use of video cameras, discreet observation, and content analysis of reports. As soon as the data-gathering method involves talking to the job incumbents (using structured interview or checklists), the job or task itself is no longer being directly studied as it is done. Techniques such as critical incident interviewing with supervisors, or technical conferences of experts, or repertory grid are all to a greater or lesser extent detached from the actual performance of the job and are therefore more open to distortion or bias. However, only by using such techniques is it possible to identify less tangible attributes or dynamic qualities which cannot be directly observed.

7 *Applicability* the job specific checklist is only applicable to

the job or task for which it has been designed. Other checklists and rating forms may have wider application. The Job Components Inventory was specifically designed for use with unskilled and semi-skilled work which might be performed by school leavers with few academic qualifications. Other questionnaires are geared to analysing managerial jobs (e.g. the Professional and Managerial Position Questionnaire). The PAQ, on the other hand, is designed to be applicable to all jobs in the economy, and interview methods based on critical incidents or repertory grid have almost universal application. If a manager is to spend time and resources developing expertise in using a number of JTR data-gathering techniques, then it would make sense to choose those that have the widest possible application rather than those that are job specific.

8 *Sensitivity* finally, JTR analysis techniques vary in the extent to which they can adequately cope with detecting and recording the less visible, discretionary aspects of jobs. By their very nature, checklists are preordained and therefore not suitable to identifying unique or unusual properties of jobs which could be critical to determining overall success. On the other hand, they do at least ensure that most aspects and activities of a job are covered. Methods which are particularly good at assessing unusual, critical, or discretionary aspects of jobs are self-descriptions, the critical incidents technique and the repertory grid approach to interviewing. These allow analysis of how an individual jobholder actually approaches problems, thinks, sets priorities, etc. The more structured and detailed the checklist is (Trainer Task Inventory, the PAQ, etc.), the greater the risk that subtle, unique, or critical aspects of a job or role will be missed.

CHOOSING DATA-GATHERING METHODS: A CHECKLIST OF THINGS TO CONSIDER

(1) What do I want to do with the results?
(2) In what form do I need the results in order to be able to achieve my objectives?
(3) What resources are available to me?
(4) Who is available to carry out the data-gathering?
(5) Do they need to be trained?
(6) How many people are available to be studied?
(7) Do I have access to jobholders, supervisors, experts, others?

13

(8) How much time do I have available to me?
(9) How much money can I spend?
(10) What information is already available?
(11) What information can be collected specially?
(12) What data-gathering methods are available to me?
(13) Will the data-gathering method be acceptable to the people involved?
(14) Is the level of language in checklists and questionnaires appropriate?
(15) Will I need to call on outside expertise (for training, for analysis of the data)?
(16) Do I need computer support?
(17) What are the best methods to use?

3
The Ten Most Useful JTR Methods

OBSERVATION

Orientation: highly task-orientated	*Sophistication:* low
Quantification: high potential	*Proximity to job:* high
Structure: adaptable	*Applicability:* moderate
Packaging: low	*Sensitivity:* low, higher for interpersonal behaviour

Brief description

Of all the JTR analysis techniques, observation of the jobholder performing the work is probably the most straightforward and readily available. At its most complex, however, it will involve completing a time-sampling checklist, which itself will have taken many hours to prepare. Whichever method is used, a great deal can be learned through observation and as such it is recommended that, wherever possible, it should form part of any JTR analysis.

(a) *Straightforward observation*

The most simple form of observation will be for analysts to position themselves so that they can view and record everything that the jobholder is carrying out. These notes may be written up at some point and used as a source of reference. This may give an analyst an overview of what the job involves, but it is not entirely satisfactory when used in isolation. For example, such analysis will not reveal the importance of any task, nor its level of difficulty; this would have to be inferred on a subjective basis by the analyst.

(b) *The observation interview*

The observation interview is a variant of the method. Here, the jobholder is observed and subsequently questioned further by the analyst in order to obtain more information on the tasks being carried out. This can be done in two ways:

(1) the analyst can observe the worker carrying out his or her duties and make a note of any areas where they feel they will need further information, and then question the worker on those topics; or

(2) the job analyst can question the worker while she or he is performing their duties, wherever this is possible.

Whichever method is used will obviously to a large extent depend on the nature of the work being analysed. For example, in a JTR analysis of brewery workers, though it *was* possible to observe the workers, because of the high level of noise in the kegging plant it was not possible to interview them while they were carrying out their work. So, once observations had been completed, the interview was conducted in a separate, quieter area of the plant. Another constraint will obviously be the pressure of the work; at moments of high pressure or tension it would be inappropriate for an analyst to interrupt the jobholder with questions. With foreign-exchange dealers, for example, it was possible on the majority of occasions to discuss with them, immediately after they had made a transaction, why they had carried it out, what the effects would be, etc. However, on those occasions when there were a large number of transactions being undertaken in a relatively short space of time it was not possible, nor would it have been appropriate, to ask questions of the dealer.

(c) *Behaviour observation*

Behavioural observation is concerned with the behaviour of the jobholder rather than the content of the tasks. Often a behavioural analysis will involve the development of a checklist of important or critical behaviours which an analyst should be looking for and concentrating on. In drawing up the checklist, Rackham and Morgan suggest a number of criteria for determining the categories of behaviour which should be included:

(1) Possibility for change, i.e. the extent to which a behaviour can actually be changed or modified at some later point. If there is no way in which the behaviour can be altered, for example by training, then there is little point in having this category in the observational analysis.

(2) Its meaningfulness, i.e. the behaviours being observed should have some relevance and meaning to the people who are being observed.

(3) The behaviour should be capable of being observed reliably and require little interpretation via the observers.

(4) Degree of differentiation, i.e. the categories must be separate and distinct from one another.

(5) Finally, relation to outcome, i.e. the category being observed should have a relevance in helping the jobholder achieve the objective of their work. If there is no relationship between the behaviour being observed and the objective of the work then there is little point in having this category in the behaviour analysis.

Obviously this requires some preparation and some knowledge of the processes being observed. Once the behaviours to be studied and analysed have been identified, they should be defined so that there is agreement amongst all analysts about what that type of behaviour involves, thus ensuring greater reliability and consistency in the results. The number of behavioural categories that are decided upon, however, should be lengthy enough to give a comprehensive overview of the job, but not so long as to make it impossible for the analyst to observe all of the categories. The final stage will be the construction of a behaviour-analysis form on which the observer can note down the number of times a behaviour occurred, when it occurred, etc.

Applications

Obviously one of the advantages of using observation is that it is readily available. It should be possible to observe all jobs for at least part of the time, and this could increase jobholders' confidence in an analyst, through knowing that the analyst will have seen them actually performing their work. Furthermore, when trained analysts are being used the process itself can be one of the most objective and it can be extremely useful for those jobs where the whole cycle of activities is observable. Finally, observation of any job can be extremely useful in providing information to an analyst who is going to conduct interviews afterwards.

Data generated

The data generated will depend upon the type of observations carried out, and when considering behavioural observation the topic of sampling arises. Two main methods of sampling behaviour exist: time-sampling and unit-sampling.

With time-sampling the observer makes a note at a predetermined interval of the activity or behaviour which is being carried out. So, for example, it may be decided that every thirty seconds the observer will record the behaviour which is being performed by the jobholder. These timings of course can vary greatly from a number of seconds up to a quarter of an hour or more.

Unit-sampling is merely making a note of a unit of behaviour whenever it occurs. This obviously relates to the categories that are contained in the observation form.

Another form of sampling is that of behaviour sequences, in which not only the frequency of each behaviour is noted but also the sequence in which it occurs. This clearly requires a much more complicated observation form and more training of the observers. An example of a behaviour-sequence form is shown in Figure 3.1.

	Behaviour sequence												
	1	2	3	4	5	6	7	8	9	10	11	12	13
Establishing needs		I							I				
Benefit statement			I							I			
Feature statement					I	I	I	I					I
Supporting				I									
Disagreeing												I	
Seeking information	I										I		

Figure 3.1 *Sequence behaviour analysis
of a salesperson at work*
(Taken from Rackham and Morgan)

18

Observational analysis results can be used in a number of ways. They can be put together in the form of a narrative, or where some form of sampling has taken place frequency counts can be given for each type of behaviour. This is especially useful for comparing the job performance of good and less good jobholders, and for identifying the ways in which performance differs. The level of analysis, therefore, can vary from being a narrative description to a very detailed quantification.

Convenience

Although observation is a readily available tool, one of the main disadvantages is that the mere fact of observing somebody affects the way in which they do their work. One way round this is to have the observer present for a long period of time so that their presence becomes less noticeable to the jobholder. An alternative is to film the person doing their work and then conduct the observational analysis on the film or video which is produced. However, the process of filming the individual could also affect their work performance.

Observation obviously works best where the activities being performed can be seen, and this is most likely where a definite sequence is involved, or in machine work etc., carried out in an accessible working environment. It is harder to undertake in the case of managerial jobs where a lot of the work being carried out is in terms of making decisions, when the processes involved are not open to observation.

Another issue is the reliability of observations. Although the process of actually recording the observations can be made reliable, there are subjective elements in other parts of the process, for example identifying the sample of behaviours to be observed and the process of interpreting results. It might be possible to obtain very reliable recordings from different observers about what went on, but their interpretations of why or how things are being carried out could differ. Rackham and Morgan found, for example, that when experts were asked to provide interpretation on the same set of data they came up with very different conclusions. One possible way round this is to present the findings of the behavioural analysis to the jobholders and ask them for *their* interpretations. Finally, the complicated forms of behavioural analysis are time-consuming, involve a great deal of preparation and require observers to be trained.

SELF-DESCRIPTION/DIARIES/LOGS

Orientation: task-orientated

Quantification: low–moderate

Structure: low

Packaging: low

Sophistication: low

Proximity to job: high

Applicability: high

Sensitivity: low, higher for interpersonal behaviour

Brief description

This method of job analysis uses any written or recorded descriptions of work provided by the jobholders themselves, including material from diaries, logs, and day-in-the-life narratives. The usual procedure is to ask an individual or a group of individuals who do the same job to record their activities over a given period.

There are three general ways in which diaries may be completed. The first is for the jobholders to record the activities in which they have been engaged at the end of a given time period on a regular basis. So, for example, they might be asked to record activities every hour or every half day. The second way is for the jobholders to make a record in their diaries every time they change from one major activity to another, and the third is for them to make a note of *specific* activities which they engage in over a period of time.

This type of exercise is reasonably easy to set up (although it depends on the cooperation of a number of people), and requires neither the constant intervention of the analyst nor their close involvement in the actual recording of information. Obviously the analyst has to be involved in briefing participants and in the results analysis which is subsequently carried out, but the actual process of recording the data is the responsibility of the jobholders. This, therefore, releases the analyst to engage in other activities, including analysing the same job using different techniques, at the same time as the diaries are being completed.

Another form of self-description is where a jobholder is asked to describe a typical day, either in an hour-by-hour format or as a narrative. This approach is extremely flexible and can be used for many different types of job, although it does assume a certain

20

literacy level on the part of the jobholder.

Applications

These types of JTR analysis work best in jobs where the tasks are not observable or where the cycle of activities is so great that it would not be practical for an analyst to be observing for any length of time. They are most suitable in the case of managerial posts where the jobholder is making decisions throughout the day which it would be impossible for an observer to pick up, but which it would be possible for the jobholder to record, identifying which decisions were made, why they were made, when they were made, etc.

Data generated

As the information is provided in narrative form, it has to be analysed by examining the content and comparing the jobholder's own descriptions with those provided by other jobholders. The use to which the information is put will depend on the objectives of the project. For example, if it is being used for selection purposes then some attempt can be made to determine skills and abilities which are required. If it is to be used for job design then it should be possible to look at the way the job is currently structured and draw conclusions as to the way it should in future be carried out. For example, a JTR project was undertaken to examine the role of pub-tenant managers, i.e. the people who supervise pub tenants, and of tenant directors, i.e. the managers of the managers, as the brewery felt that these two levels of management were not functioning as well as they ought. Amongst the approaches used was the analysis of diaries kept by a number of the managers and the directors over a given period. Information thus gathered indicated that there was a large degree of overlap in the tasks being carried out by these two levels of management: the directors, rather than supervising the managers, were in fact providing an extra level of direct supervision to the pub tenants. One of the recommendations, therefore, was that the two levels of management should be differentiated more and the roles clarified to prevent the existing degree of duplication recurring. The job restructuring would ensure that all of the necessary functions were indeed carried out.

21

Convenience

The advantages of these techniques are that they are convenient and that large numbers of people are not required to take part in a study. In fact it could work with just one person completing a diary, but in order to get a comprehensive description of a job it is better to get a number of people involved in such a project. Although the individuals themselves would need little or no training it does require their commitment to complete the diaries on a regular basis. If this is not done then obviously the data which is obtained will not be as full as it could be, which could lead to faulty assumptions and misinterpretations.

The main difficulty with this method, though, is that there may be a tendency for the jobholders to concentrate only on those areas of work which they consider to be important, thus omitting from their diaries activities which though frequent are considered less important. This could obviously create a bias or distortion of the analysis which is subsequently carried out.

JOB ANALYSIS INTERVIEWS

Orientation: task or worker-orientated

Sophistication: low

Quantification: low

Proximity to job: moderat

Structure: moderate

Applicability: high

Packaging: low

Sensitivity: high

Brief description

Interviews in this case refer to those carried out without the use of a checklist or structured questionnaire of any kind. They might include three types of interview:

(1)   the unstructured interview,
(2)   the structured interview, and
(3)   co-counselling.

In each case it is assumed that the interviewer has done at least the minimum amount of preparation for the interview – for example, looking at the job description and wherever possible observing the jobholder at work.

The unstructured interview occurs when the interviewer has no set of pre-prepared questions or a predetermined line of reasoning. Usually in this situation the interviewer will explain why the interview is being carried out, the purpose of the study, and will ask the interviewee, in general terms at first, about the work they perform. The interviewer then follows up with probing questions on particular areas in order to elicit further information. In this case the interview is rather free-flowing and is entirely dependent on the skill of the interviewer to pick up cues and to probe deeper.

With the structured interview the interviewer has a definite format in mind for the interview. This may involve going through the sequence of activities which the jobholder performs in their work, or it might take the form of an attempt to divide the work up in different ways. It should, however, be considered as an intermediate step between the unstructured interview and one which involves some form of inventory or questionnaire.

The third method, that of co-counselling, is where two jobholders are brought together and, in a sense, interview one another about the work that they carry out. Much care has to be taken in setting up an exercise such as this and it has to be explained carefully to the participants what they are doing, why they are doing it, and what is expected as a result of their discussion. The advantage of this over the traditional type of interview is that the analyst is not involved and so the participants may talk more freely. However, the disadvantage is that the jobholders themselves may well not be trained interviewers and therefore not probe areas which a trained interviewer would. Obviously, at the end of the interview some form of written statement needs to be prepared for the analysts.

Applications

Interviewing is clearly a very flexible exercise which can be applied to all levels and types of job. As long as there is someone to be interviewed then this technique can be used. It cannot be used effectively, however, in situations where a job does not yet exist and the analyst has to find out what that hypothetical job might entail. In such instances more structured techniques are necessary to focus interviewees' attention on particular aspects of the work. It *does* require the interviewers to be trained in interviewing techniques, however. Someone who is not familiar with these could well make an interviewee feel uncomfortable and, as a result, they will probably obtain far less information than might potentially be available.

Data generated

The data which is generated for interviews will usually be descriptive but could have the advantage that the jobholders themselves could be persuaded to attach levels of importance to the different types of activities which they are describing.

However, this technique has the potential of being sensitive in that a good interviewer will be able to probe the more important areas in more depth, something that a structured questionnaire or inventory would not allow to the same extent. Also it can provide an overview of the job and enables the jobholder to talk more in terms of their perceptions and feelings of the work and the environment in which it is conducted. Structured questionnaires tend not to pick up on these more affective aspects of carrying out a job.

Problems arise in combining the information from different interviews and from interviewer bias. For example, the interviewer may fail to pick up on certain areas of the work or may choose to emphasize in an interview one particular area to the detriment of others. This will obviously lead to problems in interpretation and analysis, and could lead to a distorted impression of the job.

Convenience

Overall, then, the interview can be seen as having advantages, especially in terms of sensitivity, but it should not really be used as the sole method of job analysis in any particular project. The co-counselling method has the advantage of removing the analyst from the interviewing process and enabling the jobholders to discuss the work between themselves, but it has the disadvantage that the jobholders may miss out particular areas through their inexperience of interviewing techniques. In addition, there may also be a problem in choosing people who will get on well with one another during such an interview.

CRITICAL INCIDENT TECHNIQUE

Orientation: worker orientated

Sophistication: moderate, high if computer-analysed

Quantification: can be high or low

Proximity to job: moderate

Structure: low

Applicability: high

Packaging: low

Sensitivity: high

Brief description

The process of describing and analysing critical incidents in order to get an insight into a particular process is one which is not new but which has been used by researchers and writers for many years. The actual formulation and development of the procedure, however, was carried out by J.C. Flanagan, and is a by-product of studies carried out in the Aviation Psychology Program of the United States Army and Air Force during the Second World War.

As the name suggests, it is a procedure for collecting observed incidents which have proved very important or critical to performance. To qualify as a critical incident two criteria have to be met:

(1) the incident has to be observable to such an extent that inferences can be made about the person performing the act; and

(2) it must be critical, i.e. the incident must occur in a situation where the purpose or intent of the act seems fairly clear to the observer and where its consequences are sufficiently definite to leave little doubt concerning its effects.

What emerges from this are those essentials of job performance which make the difference between success and failure in a job. The incidents are recorded in the form of anecdotes about how a person handles certain situations, and from these a composite picture of job behaviour is built up.

Flanagan has laid down the procedures that should be followed in recording incidents. These are:

(1) the general aim of the activity should be developed, and this should be recorded in the form of a brief statement, both acceptable to the jobholders and unambiguous.

(2) the people who will record the observations must be made aware of the types of incidents being sought, and therefore instructions and relevant background information must be provided. Furthermore, the interviewees should be familiar with the job that is to be studied: the best people therefore are usually jobholders or their supervisors.

(3) collect the information. Various methods can be used, the most common ones being individual interviews, group interviews, or pre-prepared record forms where the jobholder or other participants in the exercise complete a proforma, providing all of the information which is asked for on it.

The description of an incident should also follow a particular format, which is:

(1) the person should be asked to describe an incident which did or did not meet the objective.

(2) the background to the incident should be described.

(3) what the person actually *did* which was so effective or so ineffective should be described.

(4) finally, some indication should be given of when the situation occurred.

Once one incident has been obtained the process is repeated throughout the interview, or if proformas are being used the respondent will be asked to complete a number of these until they can think of no more incidents.

The critical incident technique relies to a large extent on

people's memory, and so the more recent the event the more likely it is that the person will have a good recollection of it, but there will obviously be circumstances in which it is not possible to obtain recent examples of incidents. Flanagan himself feels that the accuracy of the reporting can be judged by the detail of description which is provided. Full descriptions are an indication that the incident is being recalled reasonably accurately. Where descriptions are vague or incomplete then the less accurate the observations will be.

Rules have also been laid down for analysing the data. These break down into three major areas:

(1)   the selection of a general frame of reference which will be most useful for describing the incident. This depends upon the use to which the data will eventually be put.

(2)   category formation which, as Flanagan admits, is a subjective procedure. First of all, a relatively small sample of incidents is sorted into piles that are relevant to the frame of reference selected. Other incidents are added to these small groups and as this procedure continues so a process of redefining the categories will be required. Large categories are subdivided into smaller groups, and incidents that describe the same type of behaviour are placed together.

(3)   the level of specificity of the categories must be determined, although this will usually be constrained by practical considerations.

Applications

The Critical Incident Technique is very flexible and can be used for all types of jobs at all levels. However, as it concentrates on observable incidents and things which have already occurred, it means by definition that it is not suitable for analysing a job which does not yet exist. The technique itself has been used for many different purposes, including such things as designing personnel selection procedures, designing aircraft equipment, developing training courses, designing appraisal systems for evaluating performance, etc.

Interviewer 'Can you give me an example of an occasion when you did something extremely well (which meant that you met the objective) or when something went badly wrong and you did not meet your objective?'

Trainer: 'Yes, there was an occasion when I was running an interviewing skills training course. It had been a particularly difficult course and there were one or two tricky individuals involved. On the last day of the course a panel was carrying out their final set of interview practice. One of the difficult people was taking part in the interview and they made no effort whatsoever to appear interested, ask relevant questions or do anything a good interviewer might do. I was videoing the interview and found myself becoming increasingly angry with this person. Once their interview was finished, I went over to the panel and said that it was the worst interview that I had ever seen. The panel reacted very badly to this, as you might expect, and we became involved in an argument. There was no way that this particular group would listen to me again on the course.'

Interviewer: 'Can you tell me *exactly* what you did that was so poor?'

Trainer: 'Yes. I think the most important thing that happened here was that I allowed their behaviour to get to me and to make me feel very emotional. I allowed my feelings to show and expressed them in a way which was entirely inappropriate; I did not try to understand *why* they were behaving in that way and I did not give them the opportunity to evaluate their own performance. Instead, rather than getting them to see how bad they were in that interview, I became embroiled in a heated debate which only served to let them think I was a bad trainer.'

Figure 3.2 *Example of a critical incidents technique obtained from a trainer*

Data generated

The data obtained from a critical-incidents analysis are in the form of anecdotes or stories of the way an individual behaved on a particular occasion. It is recommended that observations are obtained from more than one group of people involved in a particular project – for example, supervisors in addition to job-holders. If the people making observations are familiar with the job then reliability is usually obtained in the types of incidents which emerge as illustrating good and poor performance. Subjectivity occurs in categorizing the incidents, and so some training of the analysts is required. It is also useful to have two people classify the same set of incidents and to compare their categories.

Convenience

The Critical Incident Technique is one which is readily available and can be relatively easily picked up by individuals with a minimum of training. The key to carrying out effective Critical Incident interviews, however, is in ensuring that the procedures are followed. In particular, analysts must ensure that the information on what the person did in each incident is described in as much detail as possible. If the behaviour of the individual is not broken down, then the subsequent analysis will be less detailed.

The one major drawback with the technique, as it is laid down by Flanagan, is that he states that hundreds of incidents at least will usually be required in order to obtain a comprehensive description of a job. Indeed, for many jobs, in particular managerial and professional positions, thousands of incidents will be needed. In our practical experience we have found that, with any one individual, it is probably unlikely that they are going to be able to provide more than ten good incidents during the course of an interview, lasting between one and one and a half hours. If the analyst has to obtain, say, 2000 incidents this means that at least 200 people have to be interviewed, which for many people is totally impractical in terms both of the time involved, and of finding such a large sample. A useful alternative procedure for carrying out the Critical Incidents is to take each of the individual behaviours which have been identified from each incident and then use these to produce the classification of behaviours. For example, from each incident it may be possible to identify five behaviours which were critical to the achieving, or otherwise, of the objective of the work. If five people have been interviewed and fifty incidents in total have been obtained, and for each incident five behaviours have been recorded, the analyst then has 250 behaviours to classify. This has proven to be an effective way of obtaining a behavioural classification, and also reduces the amount of time required to conduct such an analysis. However, it should be pointed out that only on very rare occasions have we employed the Critical Incident Technique exclusively; rather, it has been used as but one source of information, and has not been looked upon as providing *all* of the answers in any particular JTR analysis.

The Critical Incidents Technique is an interesting one to use, both for the analyst and for the people taking part. As it is anecdotes and stories that are being described, the technique can often bring colour and life into JTR analysis projects which can otherwise be rather dry in the data-gathering techniques which are used. One point to watch out for when carrying out interviews, however, is that some individuals pick up the methodology very quickly and will provide the analyst with a series of relevant incidents both good and poor. On other occasions it has been found that individuals either cannot think of relevant incidents or do not feel disposed to discuss incidents with an outsider. This is particularly the case when they have been asked to describe occasions of ineffective job performance. It is always important, therefore, to stress the confidentiality of the situation and give some indication of the ways in which the results are to be used. On other occasions, it may be the case that incidents cited tend to be ones which illustrate positive rather than negative performance, or vice versa. For example, with air-traffic controllers it was found that it was easier for them to recall incidents where things had *not* gone particularly well, because these were the ones which remained in their minds; specific occasions when work *was* being done particularly well tended not to stay in the memory because they were the norm. In analysing the data this did not prove to be a problem since the critical-incidents interviews were supported with data from other techniques.

REPERTORY GRID

Orientation: worker-orientated

Quantification: can be high or low

Structure: low but creates its own structure

Packaging: low

Sophistication: high, especially if computer analysed

Proximity to job: moderate

Applicability: high

Sensitivity: high

Brief description

The Repertory Grid is a technique which, like Critical Incidents, enables those dimensions on which good and poor performers differ to be identified. It has been developed from the Personal Construct theory of George Kelley. Personal constructs were seen by Kelley as the ways in which we view the world; they are personal because they are highly individual and they determine the way in which we behave or view other people's behaviour. The Repertory Grid is a means of obtaining these personal constructs. For a JTR analysis the objective may be to determine those constructs which differentiate the good performers from the poor, and this could be done in a number of ways. For example, if the job being analysed was that of a sales representative then the way the good representatives consider aspects of their work could be compared with the way less good representatives consider those same elements. Alternatively, a supervisor could be asked to delineate those constructs which differentiate between the good performers and the less good.

The constructs are elicited by asking the interviewees to concentrate their attention onto certain objects which are known as elements. For example, the elements for the supervisor would be the people whom he or she supervises. A number of steps would then be followed to elicit the constructs. These are:

(1) the supervisor writes the name or the initials of the people supervised onto separate cards, one for each person.

(2) the supervisor separates the cards into two piles, one for people who are good at their work and one for those who are less good.

(3) the supervisor is asked to take out two cards from the good workers' stack and one card from that of the less good. She or he is then asked to describe how the two "good" individuals are similar in the way in which they carry out their work, and how they are different from the one who is less "good".

(4) the next step involves a method called laddering, where the supervisor is probed further on that original construct in order to define it in more detail and make it more concrete. For example, if the difference between the good and less good workers was described as their motivation then the analyst would ask a follow-up question along the lines of "How do you know when a person is highly motivated?", or "What sort of things indicate a highly motivated person?", etc. Laddering in this way enables the analyst to identify very specific behaviours in detail.

(5) once the "laddering", or probing, has been completed, the cards are replaced in their piles and three more are drawn out and the process repeated. It does not matter if the same cards are taken out – the interviewee is simply asked to think of other ways in which the three individuals are similar and different. The activity is continued until the person being interviewed runs out of constructs and is starting to repeat ones which have emerged earlier in the interview. An example of a repertory-grid interview is provided in Figure 3.3.

Applications

This, too, is a flexible job-analysis technique which can be used on many different types of jobs, but it does require the interviewees to be fluent and fairly analytical in how they consider the way in which they perform their job. It is particularly helpful in obtaining information on less observable aspects of a job, such as decision-making, relationships with other people, etc.

Interviewer: 'Can you tell me something that the two people you have chosen have in common which makes them different from this third person in terms of the way they carry out their work?'

Supervisor: 'These two are very good at solving problems and identifying faults that occur with the machine.'

Interviewer: 'How can you tell that someone is good at solving problems and identifying faults?'

Supervisor: 'Well, these two are always alert, trying to identify what's wrong with the machine and deal with any faults before they become too problematic. So they avoid knocking the machine off. The third person, on the other hand, doesn't try to identify the faults, but knocks the machine off first. As a result this person's machine has a much longer down time than the machines operated by the other two.'

Interviewer: 'Are there any other ways in which you can tell whether somebody is good at problem solving?'

Supervisor: 'These two always locate the source of the problem relatively quickly — and it isn't always where the problem has manifested itself. Sometimes the actual problem may be in another part of the machine altogether. Also, they can identify the area where a problem has occurred without referring to the panel of warning lights.'

Interviewer: 'Any other ways in which you can tell when somebody is good at identifying problems?'

Supervisor: 'If you go and talk to the machine minder about the problem, the good ones will have a wider view of the problem and consider all sorts of possible alternative causes, which might include non-mechanical ones (for example, the materials they are using might not be particularly good). The less good minder always treats the faults as mechanical ones and will make guesses as to the causes and knock the machine off before analysing where the real problem lies.'

Figure 3.3 *Example of a repertory grid interview with a machine minder supervisor*

33

Data generated

The data generated from a Repertory Grid study can be analysed and examined in a variety of ways which make the study more flexible than other JTR methods. For example, at one level the behaviours which have been identified from the laddering process can be content-analysed and categorized as they stand – in much the same way as the behaviours from a Critical Incident interview. The next level, however, is to go to the preparation and analysis of an actual grid. In constructing a grid, each element is given a score against every construct, using perhaps a five-point or a seven-point scale. An example of what a grid might look like is provided in Figure 3.4. This grid can be scored manually or, as can be seen, is amenable to computer scoring and computer programs exist specifically to do this. The level of analysis will obviously depend on the use to which it is going to be put. Computer analysis is probably at its best when comparing one individual's construct system with that of another. Where one is most interested in the behaviours which are described then content analysis would probably be appropriate and sufficient.

Elements are the people supervised.

	Peter	Harjit	Helen	David	
Analyses problems carefully	3	6	6	4	Sketchy analysis of problems
Keeps machines running	3	7	7	5	Knocks machines off often
Helps others out when not busy	6	5	7	2	Doesn't help others out
Good at prioritizing	5	7	5	3	Doesn't identify correct priorities

Figure 3.4 *Example of a repertory grid completed by a supervisor of the job being analysed*

Convenience

The Repertory Grid can provide an enormous amount of data, even when only a few people are interviewed, particularly if laddering is used effectively. Training of the interviewers is required, however, because it is important that the descriptions come from the person being interviewed, and the latter should not be led or biased by the interviewer. There is sometimes a little amusement caused at the beginning of an interview when people are asked to choose cards from a pile; it often feels as if they are being invited to take part in a magician's act. But once this initial response has been overcome there are usually few problems in carrying out the interviews. Although it is the views of one individual that are being sought, it is necessary to have more than one person involved in such an exercise and also to have people looking at the job from different perspectives. For example, just to have a supervisor's view of work may not be sufficient, as the supervisor may look at a particular job in a different way from the jobholder.

The most important point which we have learnt from our experience of carrying out Repertory Grid interviews is that the laddering of a construct is the most important part of an interview. Without the laddering the analyst will be left with very vague constructs – a good worker will have a good personality and a poor worker a poor personality, a good worker will be well-organized and a poor one badly-organized. If this is all that is obtained from the Repertory Grid interviews then the time will have been wasted, as these constructs are so vague and ambiguous that they could have been identified by other means much more quickly. What the analyst needs to know in a JTR project is what does being "well-organized" actually mean, what does it describe, and what does it involve? With this information available, the analyst will be able to make far more concrete distinctions between, for example, good and poor workers, and also to define much more closely what is being sought.

CHECKLISTS/INVENTORIES

Orientation: usually task-orientated

Quantification: high

Structure: high

Packaging: high

Sophistication: low to high

Proximity to job: low

Applicability: moderate

Sensitivity: low

Brief description

The terms, job or task inventories, are often used interchangeably and usually describe a list of tasks that have to be performed for a job or a series of jobs to be completed. These lists of tasks are normally provided in the form of a questionnaire; Figure 3.5 provides an example and is taken from the Trainer Task Inventory, an inventory developed by the Manpower Services Commission and the Institute of Training and Development.

One characteristic of inventories is that they all have a number of tasks listed, which vary in type and number depending on the job. They could go from 100 up to and over 500. Another characteristic is that the tasks usually have to be rated by the respondent using a series of scales which might indicate, for example, the degree of difficulty in carrying out a particular task, the importance of carrying out a task, or the amount of time spent carrying out that particular activity. These responses are usually numerically recorded.

The questionnaires are structured and standardized, which means that large numbers of people can be surveyed for any particular JTR study, including not only jobholders but also, for example, their supervisors. Many different types of checklist or inventories exist and they are usually specific to a particular occupation or organization. However, task inventories can be used for planning purposes, for example as a guide to those having to provide education or training for people entering a particular occupation; or they can be utilized by an organization in the determination of how a particular series of jobs can be structured

Work Area 1: Identifying training/ learning needs – gathering information	Page A1			
Listed below is a task group and the tasks which it includes. Tick against all tasks which you perform. Add at the bottom any tasks you do which are not listed.	1	2	3	4
Task group	If done			
1 Design surveys				
2 Devise questionnaires				
3 Carry out surveys				
4 Construct trainee nomination forms				
5 Interview line managers				
6 Interview potential trainees				
7 Attend meetings with managers				
8 Design job description formats				
9 Carry out job analyses				
10 Carry out task analyses				
11 Write job descriptions				

Figure 3.5   A page from *The Trainer Task Inventory*
(by Morgan and Costello, MSC and ITD, 1984)

within a department. They can also be used for descriptive purposes in terms of providing an accurate description of the tasks to be performed by a jobholder and the relevant importance of different tasks in the same job. A third use of such inventories is an evaluative one, enabling jobholders to assess their own strengths and weaknesses in carrying out their work, and providing a diagnostic tool for their supervisors in assessing their performance and determining for example the training they may require.

Applications

An individual job-specific checklist is not a flexible instrument as, by its very nature, it is designed to be used to analyse only one particular type of job. As a general approach, however, it is obviously very flexible as checklists can be designed for any job requiring analysis. Checklists also provide a quantitative analysis of a job, and this can be used to determine the way in which the job may be altered in the future within the organization. It will, as a result, be possible to provide some form of analysis for a job which does not yet exist.

There are some inventories, such as the Trainer Task Inventory, which – though applicable to a particular type of job – are not necessarily specific to a particular organization. These are readily available with instructions as to how they can be used. A more detailed explanation and description of the TTI is provided below.

Data generated

Data generated from such inventories are usually very quantifiable as they are recorded in the form of ratings based on scales which have been used throughout the inventory. They are structured and can be used to provide written descriptions of, for example, the tasks which are performed, the extent to which they are performed, and their difficulty; but they can also provide very detailed numerical analysis. If large-scale surveys are being carried out, such inventories do need to be analysed by computer.

38

Convenience

Job-inventory results can be analysed to provide statistical indicators which describe task attributes and, for example, their significance to the job, or the difficulty level of each task and information on the type of person who is performing it. They can be also used to combine the information from a number of people to describe broader job activities. However, it is up to the analyst to relate the results of any task analysis to the objectives of the project. This means, therefore, that in formulating a job inventory the analyst must be quite clear why the project is being carried out and what the survey questionnaire is intended to cover. Careful preparation is thus of the essence in such work, which means it can be relatively expensive to develop. There is also the problem of determining which people to sample, particularly if there is a potentially large group from which to choose. Obviously the design of checklists needs to be thought through carefully. Furthermore, the inventories tend to be more task-orientated, making them less suitable for looking at such areas as designing selection systems, but very useful for identifying job roles – which in turn can help in organizational changes and in the development of training courses.

An example of an inventory: The Trainer Task Inventory

(Developed by Terry Morgan and Martin Costello for the Manpower Services Commission and Institute of Training and Development.)

The Trainer Task Inventory is, as its name suggests, an inventory which is relevant to trainers' jobs. It is based on a particular model of trainers' jobs which suggests that people in such work can be active in any or all of three levels, and that they can also be involved in several general functions which cut across those levels of activity. The most basic level of activity is called "Helping people to learn and develop", which refers generally to the level of direct training. This activity level is broken down into seven work areas, each of which has a particular purpose or objective – for example, to identify training/learning needs or to evaluate training.
 The second level of activity is labelled, "Helping people solve

performance problems," and is broken down into five work areas. The third level is "Helping people to anticipate needs and to formulate policies," and is divided into two work areas. Finally, there is a level labelled "General functions," and this has four work areas: administrating, managing, knowing the organization and employer's business, and self-development. Under each of the areas a number of tasks are identified, and in total the inventory contains 252 tasks. The respondent has to identify whether the task is done or not by ticking a column on the right-hand side of the page. To make this instrument flexible there are three further columns to be used by the organization in any way that is thought relevant. They could for example be employed to identify the importance of the task, to ask the respondent to think whether a particular task should be done by them if it is not already, or should not be done by them. One of the columns could also be used to ask the respondent to identify if they would like further training or guidance on a particular task. For each work area, at the end of the task statements, there are spaces for the respondents to add any tasks they perform which have not been covered by the list. This enables the list to be as comprehensive as possible.

The TTI is an interesting example of an inventory in that it provides a structure and framework to enable organizations to examine the job of a trainer. However, it is sufficiently flexible to allow analysts to use the inventory in whichever way they feel is appropriate, and to enable them to pick up aspects of the work which any totally standardized inventory would not cover.

HIERARCHICAL TASK ANALYSIS

Orientation: task-orientated	*Sophistication:* moderate
Quantification: low	*Proximity to job:* high
Structure: low	*Applicability:* moderate
Packaging: low	*Sensitivity:* low

Brief description

Hierarchical Task Analysis (HTA), developed by Annett and

Duncan, breaks down jobs or areas of work into a hierarchical set of tasks, sub-tasks and plans. The process of breaking down is performed in a very systematic way with the use of procedures and rules determining when the process should stop. The essential features of the hierarchical method of task analysis, when performed properly, are that:

(1) It is thorough and can provide very detailed descriptions of a job.

(2) It is standardized.

(3) The analysts can determine for themselves what they consider to be an appropriate level of detail, which means that there is some flexibility in the system.

(4) The results of the analysis can be directly applied in a training context, i.e. training design, course content and methods, and also the standards of performance that have to be obtained.

Task analysis is based on a number of principles which are that:

(1) Tasks can be defined in terms of objectives or end products, i.e. task analysis concentrates not so much on specific movements which are performed in a task as on what is achieved.

(2) In analysing a task, the process is one of identifying the plan needed to achieve the objective. In order to achieve the objective the jobholder will need to use a plan or strategy – whether they are aware of it or not. Any task will require a plan, and it is felt that those people who carry out the task successfully will have a suitable plan and that these are the individuals who should be talked to when carrying out an HTA.

(3) The plan for the overall goal includes a hierarchy of sub-plans and sub-goals. The behaviour that is observed when analysing a task is called an "operation", and each operation has to have a specified purpose or objective. If the objective of the action or movement cannot be identified, then it is not considered an operation. As complex plans have sub-plans, so the complex operations have sub-operations, and it is this method of breaking down tasks into hierarchies which provides the name, hierarchical task analysis.

Certain rules have to be followed in drawing up task statements and these are that they should include:

(1) An activity verb which describes in clear and concrete terms what has to be done. It should avoid ambiguous or unclear terms and phrases such as "understand" or "know".

(2) Performance standards, i.e. the level of performance which has to be obtained in carrying out an operation, should be stated.

(3) The conditions associated with task performance, which include environmental factors such as working in a cramped space or areas of high noise – or, in other words, any factor which could influence or affect the performance of the task.

The first step in using HTA is to identify the superordinate task; this is then broken down into a series of sub-tasks of perhaps four to eight. Each of these is then analysed in turn and *their* sub-tasks identified; these are written up into a form of plan or diagram which will eventually form the classic pyramidal shape of the HTA plan.

One of the acknowledged difficulties with HTA lies in determining what is an appropriate level of analysis and the amount of detail which is required. In order to assist analysts in this task HTA has a stopping rule, which consists of two parts. First, the analyst should consider what the cost would be to the overall system if that particular goal is not achieved; the second consideration is the probability that a trainee would fail to achieve the particular goal. These two factors will obviously vary from task to task and from operation to operation. The product of cost and probability of failure ($P \times C$) is the criterion which is used to decide whether to analyse an operation further. The evaluation of $P \times C$ will often be a subjective one, and since each operation has to be evaluated by this rule it will mean that the analysis will cease at different levels for different operations.

A modified version of HTA has been developed by Patrick, Spurgeon and Shepherd, and is known as Overview Task Analysis (OTA). This is a more general technique, providing a descriptive set of tasks across an area of work. One purpose is to be able to delineate tasks involved in an area of work, so that different companies or organizations can use the same OTA. As it is a more general technique, one of the main differences between OTA and

HTA is the stopping rule which is used, which determines the level of detail obtained. As a result, with OTA task breakdown stops at the lowest level at which the tasks are generalizable between companies in the same area of work.

Applications

This type of approach is best used for process or manufacturing operations where skilled, semi-skilled or unskilled workers are involved. It is most appropriate for those types of activities which are observable, follow a logical sequence, and can be determined through discussions with a jobholder. Furthermore, the job must also exist for such an analysis to take place. HTA and OTA have been used primarily to examine training content and methods, although there have been some cases of their being employed in selection situations.

Data generated

Data generated from a task analysis of this kind are usually hierarchical diagrams or tables. Hierarchical diagrams are pyramidal in shape, with the superordinate task at the top; this is then broken down into sub-tasks and each of these is broken down and this process is repeated in the diagram. An example of what such a diagram would look like is provided in Figure 3.6. Tables provide more of a narrative of the breakdown of tasks with descriptions being provided for each of them.

Convenience

The level of analysis to be undertaken will depend on the use to which the information is going to be put. It is up to the analyst to determine this: analysis can remain at a fairly general level with plans and drawings, or it can go into very minute detail. These types of interviews tend to be fairly lengthy, however, so there is a time factor to be considered, but a good detailed description of a job can be obtained from relatively few interviews. Training should be given to the analysts: this is a complex method of interviewing, requiring a great deal of patience on the part of the interviewer in terms of breaking the tasks down sufficiently well, as well as a degree of skill and experience in drawing up the plans or tables from the information obtained.

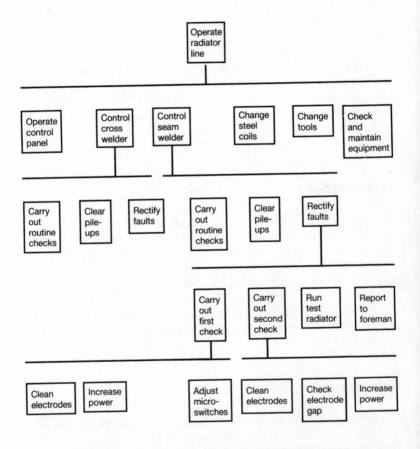

Figure 3.6 *Some operations of an assistant line operator (simplified for illustration)*
(Taken from *Task Analysis,* by Annett, Duncan, Stammers and Gray, 1979)

JOB-LEARNING ANALYSIS

Orientation: worker-orientated

Sophistication: moderate

Quantification: low

Proximity to job: moderate

Structure: high

Applicability: wide

Packaging: high

Sensitivity: high

Description

The Job-Learning Analysis is a structured job-analysis question-naire which represents a new approach to analysing jobs, being a process- rather than a content-orientated system. It describes jobs not in terms of their content or skills and abilities, but in terms of nine learning skills which contribute to the satisfactory performance of the job. A learning skill is defined as one that is used to increase other skills or knowledge. For example, we can improve our ability to observe and ask relevant questions, assess our mistakes and memorize. The learning skills represent broad categories of job behaviour which need to be learnt. They are:

(1) Physical skills, i.e. activities that require practice and repetition in order to get right/ become fast enough/ or mini-mize errors. They do not include activities which are simple procedures and can be performed easily from written or oral instructions.

(2) Complex procedures, sequences of activity or procedures which are:
    (a) remembered/memorized, or
    (b) followed with the aid of written material or other aids.

(3) Checking/ assessing/ discriminating, i.e. non-verbal inform-ation which is received by jobholders through their senses (sight, sound, smell, taste, touch) and which is used to make judgements or take some other action, and which usually takes practice to get right.

(4) Memorizing facts/ information, i.e.
   (a) information that has to be retained in one's head and recalled for brief periods of time, or
   (b) information that has to be learnt, retained and recalled for a period greater than one day.

(5) Ordering/ prioritizing/ planning, i.e. the extent to which the jobholder has any responsibility for, and flexibility in, determining the way a particular job activity is performed.

(6) Looking ahead/ anticipating, i.e. the jobholder can foresee problems and take some action which might prevent or at least reduce the effects of a problem or fault as well as meeting needs in advance.

(7) Diagnosing/ analysing/ solving, i.e. the extent to which the jobholder sorts out problems
   (a) without assistance, or
   (b) with assistance, e.g. manuals, other people.

(8) Interpreting or using written/ pictorial/ diagrammatic material, i.e. the extent to which written materials, manuals and other sources of information (diagrams, charts) need to be used/consulted in order to learn the job.

(9) Adapting to new ideas/ systems, i.e. the extent to which the jobholder is required to adapt to or learn new ideas/ equipment/methods by using manuals or other written materials, or using other sources of information.

The JLA has been designed to concentrate on the types of learning necessary for the achievement of successful levels of performance in a job because:

(1) Training frequently focuses on the more obvious activities in a job to the neglect of more subtle conceptual aspects such as adapting, anticipating and planning.

(2) It is a common experience for people completing a training course to find that they are not well equipped to do the job.

(3) Much of the material presented in training does not accurately reflect the exact conditions met by the worker *in situ*, or else the requirements constantly change and the worker needs to learn to adapt.

(4) Trainees are taught to do a specific job but do not develop the skills necessary for increasing their own skill and understanding.

Training should be designed in such a way that the process of learning becomes apparent to trainees, resulting in an increase in their capabilities to learn positively for themselves. In such cases the training will be more efficient in producing effective workers. The JLA enables trainers to design material and strategies which are appropriate for the type of learning which is required.

In conducting a JLA interview, the interviewer first of all asks the respondent to describe the main aim of the job and then asks him or her to break this down into a small number of principal activities. Next, using nine question cards (see Figure 3.7), each one probing further in a particular area of learning, the interviewer analyses each main activity in more depth, recording the outcome on specially prepared response sheets.

Each question card relates to one of the nine categories of learning and for each the analyst must elicit enough information to be able to categorize the response. There are only two response categories, "Yes" and "No", and the analyst must choose the most appropriate one for the type of learning being assessed. The analyst also records as many examples as possible under each heading. The interview usually lasts one to one and a half hours, and for most jobs only two or three interviews are necessary.

Once the interview is over, the "Yes" responses are transferred to a scoring grid which when completed shows the types of learning associated with:

(1) each of the main job activities, and
(2) the pattern for the job as a whole.

Guidance is provided in the manual on how the different types of learning can be developed through the design of appropriate training.

47

CARD 1

Q1 PHYSICAL SKILLS

Are there physical skills involved in this activity which it took you a long time to get right or become proficient in?
What are they?

Probes

How much time did it take before you got it right?
What would the consequences be if you did not perform the physical skills correctly?

CARD 2

Q2 COMPLEX PROCEDURES

In this activity, do you have to carry out a procedure or a complex sequence of activities, either (a) relying solely on memory, and/or (b) using written materials, manuals, etc?

Probes

(a) What happens if you forget the sequence or procedure?
    What are the consequences of forgetting the sequence or procedure?
(b) What written materials, manuals, etc do you use?
    How do you use them?
    When do you use them?
    How accessible are they?
    What are the consequences of not following the procedure correctly?

CARD 3

Q3 CHECKING/ASSESSING/DISCRIMINATING

In this activity, do you make adjustments/judgements based on information from your senses (sight, sound, smell, touch, taste)?
Give me some examples.

Probes

What senses, i.e. sight, sound, smell, touch, taste, do you use?
What adjustments/judgements do you make?
How do you make these adjustments/judgements?
What would the consequences be if you did not make the adjustments/judgements correctly?

Figure 3.7 *JLA question cards*

MAIN ACTIVITY No.	Description	TIME SPENT ON ACTIVITY	PHYSICAL SKILLS	COMPLEX PROCEDURES	CHECKING/ASSESSING/ DISCRIMINATING	MEMORIZING FACTS/ INFORMATION	ORDERING/PRIORITIZING PLANNING	LOOKING AHEAD/ ANTICIPATING	DIAGNOSING/ANALYSING/ SOLVING	INTERPRETING/USING WRITTEN/PICTORIAL/ DIAGRAMMATIC MATERIAL	ADAPTING TO NEW IDEAS/SYSTEMS
1.	Snack cooking, preparing and cooking meals	1/3–2/3	(1)	2	(3)	(4)	(5)	(6)	7	(8)	9
2.	Cleaning and clearing up	1/3 or less	1	2	(3)	(4)	5	6	7	8	9
3.	Serving at the counter	1/3–2/3	1	2	(3)	(4)	5	(6)	7	8	9
4.	Checking in goods, stocking vending machines	1/3 or less	1	(2)	(3)	(4)	5	6	7	8	(9)
5.			1	2	3	4	5	6	7	8	9
6.			1	2	3	4	5	6	7	8	9
7.			1	2	3	4	5	6	7	8	9
8.			1	2	3	4	5	6	7	8	9
9.			1	2	3	4	5	6	7	8	9
10.			1	2	3	4	5	6	7	8	9

(LEARNING CATEGORIES)

Figure 3.8 *The Job-Learning Analysis Scoring Grid for a catering assistant*

Applications

The JLA is most effective with jobs in the range from semi-skilled manual to skilled manual, technical and supervisory. It does not work well as a basis for obtaining a systematic description of task or job content, and it will be necessary at times to combine JLA data with the results of other analytical techniques. However, as it is a questionnaire technique with a simple response system, it *is* possible to use the JLA for jobs which do not yet exist. Furthermore, the activities being described do not have to be observable; rather they might concern whether someone has to plan ahead, anticipate problems, diagnose or analyse or solve problems, adapt to new ideas or systems, etc. Most questionnaires are designed to obtain detailed information on the content but become less useful when trying to analyse the processes involved. The JLA is intended to be an instrument which gives some indication of the processes in a fairly straightforward but helpful way.

Data generated

Two types of data are generated: the narrative descriptions, which are provided in the response sheets; and the scoring grid, which identifies the type of learning involved in a particular activity, or required for the job as a whole.

The scoring grid is straightforward to complete; the difficulties sometimes arise in deciding whether a particular type of learning applies to the main activity being questioned. The JLA and the scoring grid identify the processes of learning associated with a job, in order that appropriate ways or strategies of learning can be developed simultaneously with learning to perform the job. The JLA can, therefore, be used to identify the skills or strategies needed to learn the job activities, and then ensure that these are developed and practised by the learner. It can also be used to check the contents of a current training course, to make sure that it is providing the learner with the appropriate learning skills. The overall aim is to ensure that a trainee can not only learn the content but also be more able to assimilate new things of a similar type. For example, if a trainee canteen assistant needs to memorize the prices of different items on a menu then these should be taught – but the trainee should also be introduced to different ways of memorizing, such as grouping, associating, mnemonics, and self-testing. This will then enable them to apply effective learning methods to new items that may have to be memorized later on. Guidance is provided in the manual as to how the scoring grid and the associated notes taken from the interview can be turned into effective exercises on training courses.

Convenience

The JLA has been designed to be as straightforward to use as possible and the number of people to be interviewed need not be more than three. The time required for each of the interviews is approximately an hour to hour and a half, but time has to be given over to becoming familiar with the materials. The JLA, however, is not freely available and all people using it ought to attend a short training course on its use and interpretation. Overall, it provides information in a way that other job-analysis techniques do not in that it attempts to analyse the learning processes rather than the content of a job.

JOB COMPONENTS INVENTORY

Orientation: work-orientated

Sophistication: moderate

Quantification: high

Proximity to job: moderate

Structure: high

Applicability: moderate

Packaging: high

Sensitivity: moderate

Brief description

The Job Components Inventory (JCI) was developed to identify the skill requirements of jobs taken on by young people. As a result, the JCI has been constructed with certain features in mind, which are:

(1) That the language and concepts should be at the appropriate

level for the target group of less-qualified school-leavers.

(2) That the inventory should be easily administered by trained interviewers, not necessarily by professional job analysts.

(3) That the inventory should be comprehensive and should not take too long to administer.

(4) That the skills should be important for job performance in a wide range of occupations; the inventory should be of the kind that can be applied to curriculum development, to training and to careers guidance.

The JCI is split into seven sections. The first is an introductory section which obtains background information such as job title, details of the organization, hours of work, a brief job description, together with an outline of biographical details of the current jobholder. Section A of the JCI covers over 220 tools and pieces of equipment, ranging from small handtools such as micrometers and chisels, to larger pieces of plant such as a forge.

Section B ranges over physical and perceptual skills, consisting of 23 items dealing. for example, with strength, coordination, dexterity, reaction time and selective attention.

Section C considers mathematical skills and covers 127 aspects of mathematics up to elementary algebra and trigonometry with practical applications such as work with plans and drawings.

Section D looks at communication skill and has 22 items dealing with the jobholder's preparation of reports and letters in use for coding systems, dealing with complaints, receiving written communications and other features of interpersonal interactions.

Section E covers decision-making and responsibility, and consists of nine items including decisions about methods, order of work, standards and related issues.

Section F looks at job conditions, for example, high temperatures, work at heights, and perceived job characteristics such as a variety of tasks and feedback on work performance.

Each item of the JCI is set out on a separate page with examples and illustrations as necessary. An example of a page from the JCI is contained in Figure 3.9. The interviewer reads out from the material on each page and the responses are recorded on the response sheet in a separate booklet. It can take between 45 minutes and one and a half hours to analyse a job with the JCI, depending on the complexity of the job. An example of our own use of the JCI was concerned with machine mechanics and machine minders working on cigarette machines. In this case a comparison was to be made between the two jobs to identify the skills gaps between them. The JCI enabled a detailed analysis to be made of both occupations, and it was possible to compare the responses in each of the sections of the JCI and to identify where the major gaps between the two jobs were. Once these had been pinpointed it was possible to recommend the appropriate training to enable the minders to perform effectively as mechanics. For further details of this case study please refer to Chapter 5.

Applications

The JCI can be used for virtually all types of jobs up to supervisory level, including skilled, semi-skilled, unskilled and technical types of work. For jobs of a higher level it does not go into sufficient detail, and indeed many of the items in the JCI would be irrelevant for a managerial position. However, as it asks very specific questions in particular areas it may be possible to analyse jobs which do not yet exist or do not exist in their complete form at that moment in time. The JCI contains a large number of items, which means that it can be used on a wide range of jobs within the categories of work specified. Not all of the items will be relevant to all jobs and so the analyst must spend some time beforehand actually deciding which items it will be most relevant to discuss.

In your job do you advise or help customers or clients?

For example:
To solve a problem
To decide about buying something
To order the right spare part
To fill in a rate rebate form correctly
Any others?

What for?

How often?

☐ Never   ☐ Quite Often

☐ Occasionally   ☐ Very Often

Figure 3.9   A page from *The Job Components Inventory*
(by Banks, MSC, 1983)

Data generated

The JCI accumulates data in a number of ways. For example, in some of the items there is an inventory of, say, tools, from which the respondent can indicate those used. In addition, the respondent will have to state why she or he uses those tools – which will obviously involve some form of narrative description – and, finally, provide an indication of how often those tools are used, which will require the use of a scale. This means that the data generated will be in the form of an inventory list, narrative descriptions, and numerically quantifiable scores. As a result the data can be presented in a variety of formats, including:

(1) the skills matrix. The matrix, an example of which is given in Figure 3.10, indicates the frequency of occurrence of the skills in any particular job category, based on the frequency of use within the job. If a number of jobs are being compared, then the skills matrix provides a visual representation of the similarities and differences between the different positions.

(2) the descriptive job profile, which is a written composite job profile of the job category using information on the frequency of skills components, together with information on context within which skills are found, and the purposes for which they are used. An example of a descriptive job profile is to be found in Figure 3.11.

(3) the tools list, which is a list of all the tools which may be used in a particular job.

(4) the written sketch, which is a written case study of an individual job with the job category. This most resembles a job description containing, as it does, hours worked, people worked with, etc.

Convenience

The JCI is a straightforward JTR analysis tool which is easily understood and used with a minimum amount of training. Furthermore, research studies have indicated that it is a reliable instrument in that different people acting as interviewers analysing the

KEY:

Very frequent (large black dots) - more than 50% of jobholders use the skill very often; over 75% use the skill quite often, or equivalent combinations.

Frequent (small black dots) - more than 35% of jobholders use the skill very often; 50% use the skill quite often; or equivalent combinations.

Less Frequent (large white dots) - more than 25% of jobholders use the skill quite often; 30% use the skill occasionally; or equivalent combinations.

Blank - indicates that the skill is either extremely rare or never occurs.

Figure 3.10 *A JCI skills matrix developed for physical and perceptual skills*

Skills (rows):

- B3 Bend, stretch or reach
- B6 Finger/hand/wrist speed
- B1 Push, pull or carry heavy objects
- B8 Manual dexterity
- B9 Steady arm or hand
- B12(a) Concentration, distractions
- B12(b) Concentration, repetitive work
- B7 Finger dexterity
- B5 Arm or leg co-ordination
- B22 Good sense of touch
- B17 Distinguish shades of colour
- B2 Use of strength in short bursts
- B14 Reaction time
- B16 Close-up work
- B13 Compare similar objects
- B10 Accurate adjustments to controls
- B11 Concentrate on more than one thing
- B4 Good sense of balance
- B15 Visualize final layout or shape
- B18 Good sense of colour
- B19 Distinguish similar sounds
- B21 Good sense of smell
- B20 Good sense of taste

Job types (columns):

- PROFESSIONAL TECHNICAL
- PROFESSIONAL MANAGERIAL
- CLERICAL WITH FIGURES
- SECRETARIAL/TYPING
- CLERICAL ACTIVE
- CLERICAL WITHOUT FIGURES
- RECEPTIONIST
- CLERICAL PUBLIC CONTACT
- GENERAL CLERICAL
- SELLING
- FOOD PREPARING AND SERVING
- PERSONAL SERVICE
- HAIRDRESSING
- PRINTING AND PHOTOGRAPHY
- PAPER WORKING
- SEWING MACHINISTS
- OTHER CLOTHING MANUFACTURE
- APPRENTICE MOTOR MECHANIC
- APPRENTICE ELECTRICAL ENGINEER
- APPRENTICE MECHANICAL ENGINEER
- SHEETMETAL WORKER
- MECHANICAL ENGINEER (NON-APPRENTICE)
- WOODWORK AND JOINERY
- PLUMBING
- PAINTING AND DECORATING
- CONSTRUCTION
- REPETITIVE ASSEMBLY
- PACKING

Public contact clerical jobs (n=8)

DESCRIPTIVE JOB PROFILE

Tools and equipment

Standard office equipment is used: for example, the telephone to give clients information about insurance policies, the photocopier to copy statements and documents, calculators, weighing scales to weigh money. The job involves above average use of cash tills and below average use of the typewriter.

Physical and peceptual skills

The job involves frequent bending, stretching or reaching when filing or reaching shelves and some lifting. It also requires a lot of finger, hand and wrist speed and finger dexterity, mostly when counting out money and using a calculator. These is a need for close-up work when checking with computer printout, reading policies or other manuals. The job also involves above average concentration, when doing more than one thing at a time (for example, dealing with a customer while using a computer terminal). When counting money it is very important to be able to concentrate even if there are distractions.

Mathematical skills

The jobs all involve dealing with people about money matters (e.g., insurance, banking). To do the job, it is necessary to add, subtract whole numbers, decimals, use percentages, read charts and multiply and divide whole numbers. Less frequent but important skills include using fractions, calculating percentages, measuring weight, and multiplication and division of complex numbers and simple decimals. These skills are needed when balancing paying-in books, calculating insurance premiums, or sums to be insured. About half of the jobholders have to weigh money or use weighing machines when dealing with the post. Only some of the calculations are performed with the aid of a calculator or tables.

Communications and interpersonal skills

The communications and interpersonal skills differ considerably from other clerical jobs. In common with other clerical jobs, there is frequent need to use codes (for example, car codes), look up written information (for example, someone's insurance history), receive written information (for example, letters about stolen bank books) and to write notes, letters, memos or short reports (for example, phone messages). There is very frequent need to complete standard forms or letters (for example, bank slips, premium forms etc.) this being above average for clerical jobs. The job also demands above average interpersonal skills. Advising and helping customers or clients is very important (for example, when they open a bank account or want to take out an insurance policy), and so is receiving complaints (for example, when insurance premiums are increased). While occurring less frequently, there is above average need to negotiate (for example, when you have misquoted a premium or when arranging a no-claims discount) and to interview other people (for example, when customers have queries. In many cases this involves dealing with people over the telephone rather than face to face.

Decision-making and responsibility

The job involves more decision-making and responsibility than other clerical jobs. In three-quarters of the jobs, people are responsible for money or confidential documents which have to be locked in a safe or where other precautions are used. In more than half the jobs people decide their own order of work, this often being based on the urgency of tasks. Most people follow set procedures when deciding what tools and materials to use, although there is some choice on methods and procedures.

TOOLS LIST

Percentage of jobs using tool

Pens and pencils 100
Telephone 88
Rubber stamps 75
Scissors 63
Cash tills 63
Photocopying machine 50
Calculator 50
Weighing scales 50
Hole punchers 50
Cleaning equipment 38
Trays 38
Switchboard 38
Dictaphone 25
Duplicator 25
Adding machine 25
Trolleys 25
Glue 25
Price marker 25
Rulers 25
Staplers 25
Water heaters 25

Figure 3.11 *An example of a descriptive job profile*

57

same job have reached very much the same conclusions. Although the instrument's authors recommend that a large number of jobs be analysed, in our experience even when only a small number of people have been interviewed it has provided very valuable information. It has good face validity with people being interviewed as it manages to explore in great detail types of jobs which other job analysis techniques cannot. Also there is a great deal of flexibility in how the results can be presented, due to the variety of ways in which information is collected.

THE POSITION ANALYSIS QUESTIONNAIRE

Orientation: worker-orientated

Sophistication: high

Quantification: high

Proximity to job: moderate

Structure: high

Applicability: wide

Packaging: high

Sensitivity: low

Brief description

The Position Analysis Questionnaire (PAQ) is a structured job analysis questionnaire containing 194 job elements. Of these, 187 relate to job activities and seven of them to other information such as rates of pay, etc. The elements are organized into six divisions which are:

(1) Information input, i.e. where and how does the worker get the information used in the job?

(2) Mental processes, i.e. what reasoning, decision-making, planning, etc., is involved in the job?

(3) Work output, i.e. what physical activities does the worker perform and what tools or devices are used?

(4) Relationships with other persons, i.e. what relationships with other people are required in the job?

(5) Job context, i.e. in what physical and social contexts is the work performed?

(6) Other job characteristics, i.e. what activities and conditions other than those already described and which affect the worker are involved?

Each item or job element is rated on a specific scale which will vary depending on the item. Most of the scales used refer to the importance to the job. Others refer to the extent of use, the amount of time, possibility of occurrence and appplicability to the jobs. Examples of the most frequently used PAQ scales are provided in Figure 3.12.

CODE	IMPORTANCE TO THE JOB	CODE	AMOUNT OF TIME
N	Does not apply	N	Does not apply
1	Very minor	1	Under $1/10^{th}$ of the time
2	Low	2	Between $1/10^{th}$ and $1/3^{rd}$ of the time
3	Average		
4	High	3	Between $1/3^{rd}$ and $2/3^{rd}$ of the time
5	Extreme		
		4	Over $2/3^{rd}$ of the time
CODE	**EXTENT OF USE**	5	Almost continually
N	Does not apply		
1	Nominal/very infrequent		
2	Occasional	**CODE**	**APPLICABILITY**
3	Moderate	N	Does not apply
4	Considerable	1	Does apply
5	Very substantial		

Figure 3.12 *Examples of the most frequently used PAQ scales*

When using the PAQ, analysts must follow a certain procedure:

(1) To become familiar with the PAQ and the items.

(2) To obtain some idea about what the job entails and then use this information to eliminate those items that would not be relevant to the jobholder.

(3) To conduct the interviews ensuring that the ratings which are being given are consistent with the type of information being obtained. Very detailed guidelines on how to score the PAQ are given in the user manual.

(4) To send the completed questionnaire to PAQ Inc. in the USA to be computer-analysed.

(5) To analyse the printout which is returned from PAQ Inc.

A whole range of computer-processing options are now available. Contained in the computer is an enormous data bank which holds information on 2200 jobs, covering virtually every type of work in the American economy. As a result, normative comparisons can be made between the job being analysed and all other jobs in the economy. The type of options which are available along these lines include:

(1) Item analysis. This indicates those items or elements which have the highest percentile score, i.e. they are high when compared with all other jobs in the economy. For example, Figure 3.13 has the item analysis for a firefighter's job. The advantage of this type of analysis is that it provides a very good pen portrait of those activities which differentiate the type of work being analysed from all other types of work which could be carried out.

Items with the highest percentile scores

Name	Rating	Percentile
First Aid Cases	4.7	99
Long-Handle Tools	4.0	99
Signalling	4.0	99
Balancing	4.8	99
Temporary Disability	4.2	99
Nonprecision Tools/Instruments	4.5	99
Operating Equipment	3.0	99
Improper Illumination	2.7	99
Man-Made Features of Environment	4.2	98
Body Balance	4.3	98
Non Job-Required Social Contact	5.0	97
Awkward or Confining Work Space	2.3	97
Physical Handling	4.5	96
Assembling/Disassembling	4.0	96
Touch	3.8	96
Personal Sacrifice	3.7	95
Air Contamination	2.8	95
Estimating Size	3.7	94
Hand–Arm Steadiness	4.0	94
Level of Physical Exertion	4.0	93
Vigilance: Infrequent Events	4.2	93
Body Movement Sensing	2.0	93
Visual Displays	4.2	92
The Public	3.3	92
Permanent Partial Impairment	2.5	92
Non-Precision Tools/Instruments	4.2	92

Figure 3.13 *What are the most distinctive elements of the firefighter's job?*

(2) Dimension analysis. Factor analysis of the elements was carried out in the early stages of the research on the PAQ and it was found that 45 underlying clusters of interrelated elements emerged, thereafter termed "job dimensions". Using the information from the factor analysis, the PAQ can combine the job elements for each job and provide the job dimension scores. A full list of the PAQ dimensions can be seen in Figure 3.14.

INFORMATION INPUT

1. Interpreting what is sensed
2. Using various sources of information
3. Watching devices/materials
4. Evaluating/judging what is sensed
5. Being aware of environmental condition
6. Using various senses

MENTAL PROCESSING

1. Making decisions
2. Processing information

WORK OUTPUT

1. Using machine/tools/equipment
2. General body movements
3. Controlling machines/processes
4. Skilled/technical activities
5. Manual/related activities
6. Miscellaneous equipment/devices
7. Handling/related activities
8. General physical co-ordination

JOB CONTEXT

1. Stressful/unpleasant environment
2. Personally demanding situations
3. Hazardous job situations

RELATIONSHIPS WITH OTHERS

1. Communicating judgements
2. General personal contacts
3. Supervisory/co-ordination/related activities
4. Exchanging job-related information
5. Public/related personal contacts

OTHER JOB CHARACTERISTICS

1. Non-typical vs day schedule
2. Businesslike situation
3. Specified vs optional apparel
4. Salary vs variable basis
5. Irregular vs regular schedule
6. Job demanding circumstances
7. Unstructured vs structured work
8. Being alert to changing conditions

Figure 3.14   *PAQ dimensions*

The job dimension scores themselves are compared with all other jobs in the economy; as with the item analysis, it is thus possible to identify those dimensions that characterize this job and which differentiate it from all others. For the firefighter's job those dimensions that were above average and those that were below average are shown in Figures 3.15 and 3.16.

RESULTS: JOB ANALYSIS (PAQ) INTERVIEWS

The firefighter's job is EXTREME in its demands in the following areas:

Dimension No.		Percentile
5	Being aware of environmental conditions	98
22	Being in a stressful/unpleasant environment	94
24	Being in hazardous job situations	94
10	Performing activities requiring general body movements	93
32	Being alert to changing conditions	90

Overall Dimensions

44	Working in unpleasant/hazardous/ demanding environment	97

Extreme = 90th percentile or higher

Figure 3.15 *How does the firefighter's job compare with other jobs?*

RESULTS: JOB ANALYSIS (PAQ) INTERVIEWS

The firefighter's job is ABOVE AVERAGE in its demands in the following areas:

Dimension No.		Percentile
16	General physical co-ordination	87
29	Working an irregular schedule	77
13	Performing controlled manual and related activities	76
11	Controlling machine/processes	71
23	Engaging in personally demanding situations	68
1	Interpreting what is sensed	65

Overall Dimensions

41	Engaging in physical activities	84
40	Being aware of working environment	77

Above average = above 60th percentile

Figure 3.16 *How does the firefighter's job compare with other jobs?*

(3) Scores on selected human attributes, such as arithmetic reasoning or capacity to deal with time pressures, needed to perform the work, can also be provided – once again on a normative basis.

(4) Estimates of aptitude requirements can be made by reference to a data base on which both PAQ analyses and General Aptitude Test Battery (GATB) validation studies have been conducted. The PAQ provides the estimated average and minimum aptitude test scores on the GATB of workers in the position being analysed. Furthermore, the PAQ can provide such information as interrater reliability and data verification, i.e. checking the scores are consistent throughout the questionnaire.

Applications

The PAQ has been used to analyse jobs ranging from the most basic manual task to the most high-ranking management position. As such it is extremely flexible and versatile, and has possibly the greatest coverage obtainable from a structured questionnaire. Also, as the information provided is in numerical format it is possible to question people using the PAQ about jobs which do not yet exist and to obtain a computer printout giving an initial description of the dimension scores for that job. This can then be compared with jobs that already exist within the organization and some attempt made to define the job so that it fits well into the existing structure of the organization.

Data generated

Because of the complexity of the analysis involved with PAQ data it must be processed by computer. However, there are a vast range of options available, which obviously means that if best use is to be made of the PAQ some knowledge and acquaintance with these different options is important. The one drawback with the information generated is that actual job descriptions are very difficult to obtain, unless detailed notes are kept during the interview in addition to the scoring.

Convenience

The most powerful reason for using the PAQ is the computer-processing options which are available and the "world of work" comparisons which can be obtained, enabling an analyst to identify, normatively, where the job being analysed fits in amongst all other jobs. Also, only five people have to be interviewed in order to obtain good reliability from the data. Training is required of analysts because the questionnaire is complicated and the manual instructions complex. The actual materials needed to carry out a PAQ interview are relatively cheap and easily available, but of course for users in the United Kingdom there is the added cost and delay of mailing material to the United States to be computer-analysed.

Our own use of the PAQ would indicate that it is extremely good for providing a very broad brush picture of a job, but that if more detail is required then other techniques which highlight certain areas need to be used in addition – for example, the Repertory Grid or the Critical Incidence Technique.

Furthermore, the PAQ tends to be most useful for those jobs that are distinctive in some way or other, such as firefighter or air-traffic controller. Although the PAQ has been used on all types of occupation there is a top and tail effect in that jobs at the higher levels (which involve a great deal of decision-making and allow for a lot of discretion on the part of managers), and those at the semi-skilled or manual level (where a lot of tools and equipment are involved and where there are many physical operations, but the decisions being made are not very complex), are not adequately covered. In such cases, other techniques which can provide the required information should be used to support the PAQ, or even *instead* of it. For example, for manual semi-skilled jobs a better description of the work would probably be obtained from an inventory such as the Job Components Inventory. Furthermore, a professional and managerial version of the PAQ, known as the Professional and Managerial Questionnaire (PMPQ), has been developed, and implicitly indicates that the PAQ does not pay sufficient attention to areas of work such as decision-making, planning, prioritizing, etc.

4
Eight More JTR Methods

There are many other job analysis techniques available and the following list provides some information on a few of them, but does not go into as much detail as the ten methods described in Chapter 3.

PARTICIPANT OBSERVATION

Orientation: worker-orientated

Sophistication: moderate

Quantification: high

Proximity to job: moderate

Structure: high

Applicability: moderate

Packaging: high

Sensitivity: moderate

Participant observation is where the analysts become involved in doing the work for themselves, so rather than observing or interviewing the jobholder they themselves actually carry out the tasks. The advantage of this is that it gives the analyst a flavour of what it feels like to do the work and some idea of the stresses and strains it imposes on the jobholder. Obviously one major drawback is that the observation can only be undertaken in those situations where the consequences of a mistake are not very serious. For example, sorting out letters in a postal sorting office where an error, although it might slow things down, can easily be rectified. Participation can also involve the analyst in the training courses in some way. This occurred during a firefighting job analysis where it was possible to try out some of the equipment which firefighters use and to observe them going through certain of their training procedures. However, it would have been totally impossible for an untrained analyst actually to take part in a real firefighting situation, even if he or she wanted to.

CONTENT ANALYSIS

Orientation: task or worker-orientated		*Sophistication:* low	
Quantification: can be high or low		*Proximity to job:* can be high or low	
Structure: can be high or low		*Applicability:* low	
Packaging: low		*Sensitivity:* moderate	

When preparing a JTR study an analyst should always consider what documentation is available and wherever possible study this before any actual interviewing or observation takes place. Documentation here can include things such as job descriptions, person specifications, appraisal forms, etc.

However, in some circumstances even more information may be available; it might include performance appraisals – so it might be possible to compare less good workers with good ones, and identify those dimensions that differentiate between them. It might also be possible to look at the product of the work, the type of manuals that jobholders have to look at, the kind of diagrams that they have to analyse or draw, etc. Another source of information is the content of training courses, such as training manuals, and the topics that are covered on a training course. The latter will obviously provide information as to what the trainers explicitly and implicitly see as being important to teach. In a job analysis of workers in catering units of a regional transport authority the training documentation provided a rich source of information, giving an initial indication of the types of areas of work that were seen as being important or crucial to performance. Once the analysis had been completed it was possible to compare the results of the JTR study with what was in fact being taught on these courses and make appropriate recommendations.

Finally, there may also be information on previous job analysis or job evaluation studies. In the JTR analysis of air-traffic controllers a variety of documentation was available, including performance appraisal reports, research studies from Britain and

and the USA, and air-miss reports. The latter document occasions when aircraft had an air- (or "near" miss). It was possible from these to identify those air-misses for which the primary responsibility lay with the air-traffic controller, and to pinpoint what the controller had done in that situation that had led to the incident. This was in effect a form of critical-incidents method, enabling us to cross-validate the information given to us by air-traffic controllers in the critical-incident interviews.

EXPERT CONFERENCES

Orientation: worker-orientated	*Sophistication:* low
Quantification: low	*Proximity to job:* high
Structure: low	*Applicability:* low
Packaging: low	*Sensitivity:* moderate

On occasions it may be useful to bring together a group of people who are familiar with the job being analysed, although they may not be the jobholders themselves. They might include trainers of people in those positions, selectors, supervisors, designers of the equipment used, etc., and from the ensuing discussion one can try to glean what they see as being the main characteristics required of the jobholder. This could be formalized more by using the Critical Incident Technique for example, or through the use of Repertory Grid. The expert conference method, however, should not be a substitute for talking to jobholders; after all, the people who know most about the job (i.e. who are most expert) will be the jobholders themselves. Indeed on many occasions it is worth while returning to the jobholders at some point with the results of the job analysis study to gain their views and their interpretation of the results and conclusions.

WORK PERFORMANCE SURVEY SYSTEM

Orientation: task-orientated

Sophistication: high

Quantification: high

Proximity to job: high

Structure: can be high or low

Applicability: high

Packaging: high

Sensitivity: moderate

This is a technique developed by Sidney Gael of AT&T (American Telephone and Telegraph Company). The Work Performance Survey System (WPSS) was designed to produce information which could assist managers in making human-resource planning decisions, and which also could improve the implementation of tailor-made job inventories, which in turn provide quantitative data about tasks performed by people within the company, and which could be analysed on easy-to-use computer programs. It has to be understood that AT&T is an enormous company, and that one of the reasons for having such an inventory was to determine the way in which a given job was being performed in different parts of the organization and in different locations. WPSS is a good technique to use when:

(1) Numerous employees perform the job to be analysed.
(2) A large sample of those employees is expected to provide data about their work.
(3) The desired sample works at a number of different plants.
(4) Quantitative job data are required.
(5) A high degree of specific information is required.
(6) The type and volume of data anticipated will require computer analysis.

A number of techniques are recommended for deriving task statements for the jobs under analysis, including observation of jobholders, content analysis of materials which relate to the work, interviews with jobholders, supervisors, and other people who are knowledgeable about the job and – in particular – specially

69

developed WPSS questionnaires which provide information about tasks and functions performed by jobholders. The job information obtained is used to compile a list of the tasks undertaken by jobholders, and this list becomes the main part of the WPSS questionnaire. The questionnaire is given to jobholders, who rate the task statements for significance specifically by reference to:

(1) the importance of the task to overall job performance,
(2) the frequency with which the task is performed, and
(3) difficulty of performance.

The rating scales are carefully anchored and the data generated are analysed using a specially developed suite of computer programs, making the system extremely flexible and easy to use. Of course, although the questionnaire was designed to maximize flexibility, especially in how the data are collected and analysed, nevertheless the way the information is entered into the computer, stored and retrieved, is done in accordance with very specific rules.

Summing up, the WPSS is a valuable addition to the line of job inventories. Particular drawbacks of its techniques include the amount of time it takes to complete such a survey, but the advantages are that it is flexible and that the procedures for drawing up the task statements are very rigorous. It also has a range of computer options available to analyse the data obtained. As mentioned earlier, however, it is best used for large-scale surveys rather than the small-scale JTR analysis.

COMBINATION JOB ANALYSIS METHOD (C-JAM)

Brief Job Analysis Method (B-JAM)

Orientation: worker-orientated	*Sophistication:* low
Quantification: moderate	*Proximity to job:* low
Structure: moderate	*Applicability:* wide
Packaging: low	*Sensitivity:* moderate

Combination Job Analysis Method, or C-JAM, has been developed by Edward Levine. It is not intended to be a sophisticated job analysis method but will provide useful information for managers. The aim was that the people using it would find the results comprehensible and that they would not need to have a great understanding of statistics in order to analyse the results. Also, the technique is intended to be versatile to meet the many different needs that a manager might have for using a job analysis.

Task statements are developed: the knowledge, skills, abilities and other personal characteristics (KSAOs) needed to perform the tasks are evaluated and rated in relation to their importance to job performance. The statements are generated during meetings of job experts who might include jobholders, their immediate supervisors, and others familiar with the job being analysed. There are guidelines laid down as to the characteristics a task statement should have. Alternatively, task statements can be derived from individual interviews and other relevant personnel. The list of task statements is then reviewed and duplicate ones are removed, which should leave a draft list of between 30 to 100 task statements, which are then organized and categorized into major duty or function categories. The next step is for the tasks to be rated by a group of job experts, which could be the same group that participated in the earlier meeting or a new one. Tasks are evaluated using three scales which cover:

(1) the relative time spent on each task,
(2) the difficulty of the task, and
(3) its criticality.

A task importance value is then calculated using the following formula: Task importance value = difficulty × criticality + time spent ratings. This process is repeated for all of the tasks that have been rated. At the end, it should be possible to organize the lists of tasks within their categories in order of importance.

The next step is to determine the employee's attributes needed to perform the tasks generated. These employee characteristics are grouped under characteristics of knowledge, skills, abilities and other personal characteristics, i.e. KSAOs. The group of experts are then asked to generate KSAOs for the total job and for each functional category, one at a time. The objective is to obtain between 30 and 100 KSAOs. These are then reviewed and rated by the group, the scales used being:

(1) whether the KSAOs are necessary for newly hired employees,

(2) whether it is reasonable to expect to find the KSAO in labour markets,

(3) the extent to which trouble will occur if the KSAO is ignored in selection, and finally

(4) the extent to which different levels of the KSAO distinguish the superior from the average worker.

These ratings are next analysed and the final product is a complete list of all KSAOs with accompanying ratings.

This method has been developed primarily for personnel selection and training; the pattern of ratings on the KSAOs will give some indication as to whether they are to be used for selection or training and how they are to be used for each of those applications. For a KSAO to be used in a selection situation it has to have met three criteria. The majority of experts must have voted that the KSAO is necessary for newly hired workers, is practical to expect in a labour market and, thirdly, the average rating on likely trouble is not too low. Other guidance is given as to how the KSAOs can be used in training situations.

A modified and streamlined version of the C-JAM is provided in the Brief Job Analysis Method or B-JAM. This is intended to be used where selection or training is about to begin immediately and the deadlines are extremely tight. Obviously the B-JAM will not be as thorough as the C-JAM but it does provide a useful framework for obtaining job analysis information.

However, very little training is required in order to be able to carry out the analysis. The one drawback of a technique of this kind is in attempting to reach some sort of consensus or majority view about what KSAOs should be included as part of the selection criteria. Just because a majority of people agree that a KSAO should be included does not necessarily make it justifiable or correct. For example, it can be envisaged that many people would automatically include educational qualifications as part of their person specification, whereas on some occasions they may not be necessary or justifiable at all. Nevertheless, B-JAM would appear to be a practical method which is not very time-consuming.

FUNCTIONAL JOB ANALYSIS

Orientation: task- and
worker-orientated

Sophistication: high

Quantification: high

Proximity to job: low

Structure: high

Applicability: wide

Packaging: low

Sensitivity: moderate

Functional Job Analysis (FJA) was developed by S. A. Fine and is a comprehensive approach which focuses on interactions between the work, the workers, and the work organization. Tasks which describe what a worker does and what gets done on a job are defined as "an action sequence grouped through time designed to contribute a specified end result to the accomplishment of an objective and for which functional levels and orientation can be reliably assigned". Task statements, as in other techniques, must follow a particular format, and the steps involved in gathering task information include the analysts becoming familiar with the jobs, and then interviewing sufficient people to get coverage of the tasks which are performed. The task statements should next be written, according to given rules, and then verified and reviewed by a group of experts who add any statements which they feel are missing.

The task statement format includes an action verb to describe the actions taken, the purpose of the action, and the tools, method, and/or equipment used.

Each task is then rated and analysed on seven scales: three Worker Function Scales of Data, People and Things (DPT); the Worker Instruction Scale and three General Educational Development Scales of Reasoning, Mathematics and Language. In addition, each scale has a number of levels and each statement is rated on these worker functions and a task bank prepared. Each statement is written onto index cards which contain the level scores and also the Worker Function Orientation scores, i.e. the percentage of the worker's involvement in the performance of a task that deals with data, people and things. The sum of the three percentages must equal 100%. A typical task bank will include 50 to 60 task statements.

SCALE NAME	DESCRIPTION
Data	The way the worker relates to information, ideas, facts and statistics
People	The way the worker interacts and communicates with people
Things	The way the worker physically interacts with machines, tools, equipment, etc
Worker Instruction	The amount of discretion and prescription the worker has
Reasoning Development	The reasoning required in the work
Mathematical Development	The level and kind of mathematical ability required
Language Development	The level and kind of verbal ability required

Figure 4.1 *Details of each of the scales used in the FJA*

The next stage is the development of Performance Standards Tasks Statements which are a criterion for assessing the results of a worker's tasks, and the Orientation percentages provide the basis for determining descriptive as well as numerical performance standards. The FJA can also be used in the development of training content, distinguishing among three types of skills:

(1) Functional competencies that enable an individual to relate to DPT.

(2) Specific competencies that enable an individual to perform specific tasks according to the standards of a particular organization.

(3) Adaptive competencies that enable an individual to adapt and use functional and specific content skills in a given situation.

This is a very flexible technique which provides detailed information on both tasks and abilities. Its flexibility means that it has a wide range of applications including job and career design, developing selection procedures, designing training courses, etc. However, it is a very time-consuming process to develop the task bank and obviously training and knowledge of the technique is required by analysts. Once the task bank has been developed, though, the analysts will find they have a source of information which they can return to and use for a variety of purposes; as long as the task bank is kept up-to-date, FJA will repay the investment time for many years ahead.

THE JOB ELEMENT METHOD

JOB ELEMENT EXAMINING

Orientation: worker-orientated

Quantification: moderate

Structure: moderate

Packaging: low

Sophistication: high

Proximity to job: low

Applicability: wide

Sensitivity: moderate

This method was developed by E.A. Primoff and focuses on worker traits, ignoring tasks or actual job behaviours. The worker characteristics are known as knowledges, skills, abilities and other personal characteristics or KSAOs. These are the job elements from which the method gets its name. A job element may be:

(1) A knowledge, such as knowledge of accounting principles.
(2) A skill such as skill in woodworking tools.
(3) An ability, such as an ability to manage a program.
(4) A willingness such as a willingness to do simple tasks on a repetitive basis.
(5) An interest, such as an interest in learning new techniques.
(6) Personal characteristics, such as reliability or dependability.

The method involves having a number of experts who are familiar with the job; these might include jobholders, supervisors, and other knowledgeable people, and they are asked to describe the KSAOs needed to perform the work. Each of the elements is then rated by the experts on four scales, which are:

(1) Barely acceptable, i.e. what proportion of even barely acceptable workers possess the element?

(2) Superior: how important is the element in differentiating between the good and the less good worker?

(3) Trouble: how much trouble is likely if the element is ignored when choosing applicants?

(4) Practical: how practical is it to expect applicants to the post to have a particular KSAO?

Analysis of the ratings is then carried out and the following values are calculated:

(5) Total Value, i.e. this determines whether an item is broad and so can be considered to be an element, or is narrow, and so is a sub-element.

(6) Item Index, i.e. the extent to which a sub-element is a useful factor.

(7) Training Value, i.e. an indication of those elements or sub-elements that might be valuable areas for training.

Through the analysis of the ratings, a list of the most critical eight to twelve KSAOs is determined. Some will be used in personnel selection and others identified for particular use and attention in training programmes that are developed.

Job element data can be used as a basis for developing an examination or a "crediting plan" for a specific job. A crediting plan describes the level of KSAOs required to perform the job and is used to assess the applicant's abilities, qualifications, etc. It is developed from elements identified during the rating process with some additional input from job knowledge experts. Some elements may be used for tests in order to rank applicants for jobs, others may be used on a pass/fail basis.

The job element method has been developed specifically as a worker-orientated one and has not paid much attention to task or functional analysis. However, a modified form of job element method is available which does provide more information about the actual tasks involved in the job. This technique has also been influential in providing ideas for the format of other job analysis techniques, e.g. the use of experts in brainstorming sessions, using four factor-rating schemes and the concept of the crediting plan.

ABILITY REQUIREMENT SCALES

Orientation: worker

Quantification: high

Structure: high

Packaging: moderate

Sophistication: high

Proximity to job: low

Applicability: high

Sensitivity: low

As with the Job Element method the Ability Requirement Scales also concentrate on the characteristics of the person needed to perform a job rather than the actual tasks involved in the work. However, they differ from the Job Element method in that they rely on a predetermined list of 37 human abilities, prepared by E.A. Fleishman. The abilities are designed to provide a way of specifying the individual differences in worker performance and learning ability, and should be applicable to all tasks. An ability is defined as a general human trait that makes some people better performers than others in groups of related tasks. The abilities are grouped into four categories:

(1) Mental ability such as verbal comprehension.

(2) Physical ability such as stamina.

(3) Psycho motor ability such as choice reaction time, i.e. the speed of response of an individual when presented with a particular signal.

(4) Abilities having to do with the way sensory material is perceived such as spatial orientation.

The scales used in rating the abilities, then, are the Ability Requirement Scales, which are five- or seven-point rating scales. Each scale is anchored with examples of tasks that would indicate relative comments on the ability required for the different tasks.

Each of the abilities is defined in detail and descriptions given as to how each one differs from others which appear to be similar. Then a rater will either look at the job as a whole, or take each individual task and rate the level of each of the 37 abilities which are required for that task or for the whole job. A large number of raters is required for this process but the end result is that 37 ratings will have been made for each task (i.e. one for each of the abilities). The analysis will also provide the average ratings on the level of each ability required for performing the job.

Task generation, or task description, is not a part of this method – it is looking exclusively at abilities, and as such is a worker-orientated method.

5
JTR Case Studies

CASE STUDY 1

JTR Analysis and the Introduction of New Selection Procedures:

Background

The Civil Aviation Authority had used paper-and-pencil tests as part of the selection of *ab initio* air-traffic control cadets for a number of years. Although the standard of air-traffic control officers (ATCO) who successfully qualified was very good, there was an unacceptably high drop-out rate from the training courses. It was felt that a JTR analysis was required of the air-traffic controllers' posts in order to identify a new selection procedure which could be introduced in order to reduce the drop-out rate. The formal objectives of the project were:

(1) To conduct a formal job analysis so that relevant and reliable selection criteria could be specified.

(2) To devise a paper-and-pencil test battery that would predict success as an ATCO.

(3) To suggest areas for further study that might lead to practical tests to improve on the predictive power of the test battery.

Design of the study (See Figure 5.1)

The study was designed to enable the consultants to:

(1) become familiar with the job,
(2) describe what actually takes place, and
(3) identify the critical components that tend to separate good controllers from less good ones.

Future needs and technical changes would also be taken into account. The information, obtained from diverse sources, would

79

form a basis of hypotheses about the selection of ATCOs which would then be tested in the validation phase of the project.

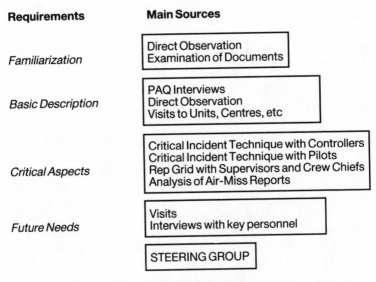

Requirements	Main Sources
Familiarization	Direct Observation Examination of Documents
Basic Description	PAQ Interviews Direct Observation Visits to Units, Centres, etc
Critical Aspects	Critical Incident Technique with Controllers Critical Incident Technique with Pilots Rep Grid with Supervisors and Crew Chiefs Analysis of Air-Miss Reports
Future Needs	Visits Interviews with key personnel
	STEERING GROUP

Figure 5.1 *Structure of the Job Analysis Project*

The techniques that were chosen were dependent entirely on the needs of the project. Because this was a very technical job, it was important that the analysts spent time becoming familiar with it. Therefore, observation interviews were carried out which involved the analyst sitting next to an air-traffic controller, with their own headsets (so that they could listen to the conversations between the ATCOs and the pilots), taking notes during the observation period and, whenever it was possible, asking the ATCOs what they were doing, why they were doing it, how they had made their decisions, etc.

Also, part of the familiarization included the examination of documents and a literature review on previous research on ATCOs. Visits were made to different units where ATCOs are based, and PAQ interviews were carried out.

In terms of identifying the critical aspects of the job and those characteristics that distinguish the less good from the good, the critical-incident technique was used, both with controllers and

80

with pilots, who are the users of the service. Furthermore, repertory grid interviews were carried out with supervisors of air-traffic controllers and crew chiefs. Finally, an analysis of air-miss reports was conducted and particular emphasis was placed on those misses that had been identified as being the responsibility of the air-traffic controller.

To determine future needs, interviews were carried out with key personnel and other researchers who had been involved in developing new equipment for air-traffic controllers.

Data gathering

The data gathering itself was spread over a four-month period. Most of the interviewing was conducted with ATCOs, using either the observation interview, the PAQ, or the Critical Incidents Technique. However, given the critical nature of this job, a wide range of other people were also seen during the course of the project, including the supervisors of ATCOs, the crew chiefs, pilots, engineers and researchers.

Results

The findings from the various techniques were synthesized into an overall model of ATCO work and this was used to specify selection criteria. Some examples are provided here to illustrate the kinds of information that contributed to the model.

Figure 5.2 shows the items from the PAQ checklist with scores above the 90th percentile. In other words, these items are more important or have to be performed more often in ATCO work than in 90% of all the jobs in the economy. As can be seen, aspects such as "vigilance for continually changing events", "providing non-routine information", "time-pressure", "decision-making" and "combining information" all emerged as very important aspects of this post.

The results of the critical-incidents interviews with ATCOs and supervisors can be seen in Figure 5.3. The critical-incident interviews with ATCOs were supplemented with identical interviews with pilots, and also with the analysis of air-miss reports. As can be seen, there was a great deal of overlap in the types of incidents obtained and the categories of behaviour identified from each of these three sources.

Visual displays
Licensing/certification required
Negotiating/agreeing terms
Vigilance: continually changing events
Advising
Sitting
Non-routine information exchange
Time pressure of situation
Decision-making
Combining information
Short-term memory
Estimating time
Supervision received
Vigilance: infrequent events
Recognition

Figure 5.2   *PAQ Items scoring above the 90th percentile
for both Area and Tower Controllers*

Air-Miss Reports	Pilots	ATCOs
Handover	–	–
FPS	–	FPS
Communication	Provision of information	Communication
		Confidence
–	–	
Mental picture	Lack of awareness	–
Faulty assumptions	Anticipation of events	Anticipation of events
Concentration/distraction	Concentration	Concentration/distraction
Indecisveness	Decision-making	Decisiveness

Figure 5.3   *Critical Incident Categories from air-miss
reports, airline pilots and ATCOs*

The repertory grid analysis revealed that supervisors and crew chiefs are prepared to rank order controllers in terms of the way they do, or approach, the job. In evaluating quality of performance, the supervisors placed a great deal of emphasis on professionalism and attitude generally, as well as on cooperativeness and teamwork, which did not emerge as such an important feature from other sources in the analysis. Attribute profiles and PAQ dimensional scores were analysed separately for airport controllers and area controllers in order to identify whether there were any significant differences between them. As Figure 5.4 shows, there were many similarities between the two jobs but there were some dimensions on which they varied significantly. On presenting these results to the CAA, it was felt that these were genuine and explainable differences.

	PERCENTILE	
	AREA	TOWER
Communicating judgements and/or related information	90	74
Being alert to changing conditions	90	78
Using machines, tools, or equipment	83	72
Processing information	78	62
Working in a businesslike situation	78	87
Making decisions	77	77
Using various sources of information	75	84
Interpreting what is sensed	74	72
Working on an irregular vs regular schedule	74	81
Engaging in personally demanding situations	73	61
Exchanging job-related information	63	66
Performing unstructured vs structured work	60	93
Performing co-ordinating or related activities	57	76
Being aware of environmental conditions	52	84

Figure 5.4   *PAQ dimensions above average for both positions*

From the diverse information obtained using the different methods of job analysis, it was possible to formulate a tentative model of the core skills required by ATCOs, together with contextual and temperamental factors affecting them (Figure 5.5).

Core skills	Ability to absorb information simultaneously from multiple sources
	Ability to absorb new information while making decisions
	Ability to project forward on the basis of current information
	Ability to adjust constantly the whole picture

Contextual factors	Speed of decisions
	Sporadic time pressure
	Sudden high-level demands on the individual
	Distractions
	Fluctuations between routine and non-routine
	Checking/up-dating information
	Short-cycle repetitive work

Temperamental factors	Readiness to work within a system
	Preference for working to set standards
	Co-operativeness
	Convergent thinking
	Decisiveness and confidence
	Conscientiousness
	Structured thinking
	Self-control

Figure 5.5   *Tentative model of ATCO core skills*

Core skills are defined as the abilities essential to performance as an ATCO. Conextual factors represent aspects of the ATCOs' working environment that affect the way in which the core skills are used. Finally, temperamental factors represent characteristics

of the individual which are associated with satisfactory performance of the core skills, taking into account the contextual factors.
The job analysis revealed four core skills:

(1) The ability to absorb information simultaneously from multiple sources. This can be seen to be the opposite of tunnel
vision and would seem to involve sensory alertness and a
wide attention span.

(2) The ability to absorb new information while making decisions. This is related to the capacity to receive and absorb
information about aircraft which will be relevant to later or
even imminent decisions while other decisions are being
made, or while other information is being received or given
by the controller.

(3) The ability to project forward on the basis of current information. As traffic situations are constantly evolving and
changing it is essential for ATCOs to plan and think ahead
and not become preoccupied with immediate decisions. Some
decisions made by a controller may be adequate for the
immediate situation but a different decision might be more
efficient if the controller was thinking ahead.

(4) The ability to adjust constantly to the whole picture. From
many sources in the job analysis the ability to form a mental
picture or have a total grasp of the situation emerged as crucial to satisfactory performance. The picture is constantly
changing and it is probably the contextual factors such as the
time pressure and distractions rather than the picture's
complexity that make the formation and adjustment of the
picture a critically difficult task.

The core skills were obviously not used in isolation; they were
really different aspects of the overall task being performed by controllers, and had to be seen in context. Decisions had to be made
quickly, and the time pressure (which is usually sporadic rather
than continuous) made the skills much more difficult to perform.
The significance of these and the other contextual factors varied
according to where the controller was working – he or she might
be the area controller in a sector which is busy almost all of the
time or operating at an airfield where there are only a few movements a day. in terms of selection, however, the standards set
obviously needed to veer towards the most complex and difficult

85

when taking the contextual factors into account.

The other contextual factors in the model are the necessity of working in a noisy distracting environment; the possibility that at any moment an emergency may make sudden and extreme demands on the controller (particularly during a quiet phase); and the routine and repetitive nature of much of the work with a short-cycle span covering the time a plane enters the ATCO's control to the point it leaves. The remaining factor was the need to check and update information. This is mostly done by means of Flight Progress Strips and the checking and amendment of these is crucial. The actual skill-level involved is not very great, but speed and accuracy in checking numbers and letters are likely to save valuable thinking/talking time. It is therefore included as a contextual factor because the information on the strips is a key component of the controller's job.

The temperamental factors emphasize the importance of the individual controller working within a tightly defined system with set standards, fixed procedures, and for the most part standardized language. In terms of problem-solving, convergent (as opposed to divergent) thinking is required, in that the solution is usually one of several well-defined possibilities rather than one that requires originality or creative thinking. It was likely also that controllers needed to be capable of thinking in a structured or concrete way rather than abstractly. Finally, high degrees of conscientiousness, self-control, and decisiveness are required so that decisions can be made quickly.

Use of the results

The JTR analysis findings permitted the development of a more precise person specification, which assisted interviewers in the first round of interviews. Although a simulation was thought to represent the best method of assessing the core skills, it was possible to recommend, from the PAQ attribute profile and the critical incidents results, pencil-and-paper tests that would measure some of the required aptitudes.

The JTR results were also used as the basis for the development of a job-performance rating scale during a subsequent concurrent validation study which confirmed the value of the tests.

Key points

(1) The use of a variety of techniques and the obtaining of a variety of viewpoints enabled a detailed model to be developed for a very key position.

(2) The analysis, moreover, enabled not only the skills and abilities to be identified, but also those factors in the environment that could impair or impede job performance.

(3) By referring to the model it was possible to devise a trial test battery, plan the validation study, and specify the criteria that would be used in the evaluation of job performance.

CASE STUDY 2

Analysis of Organizational Culture: The use of critical incident and JLA interviews to identify core selection criteria

Background

A major energy company was constructing a new plant in a green field site to blend, package and distribute lubricants. The new plant represented a major shift from a low-technology, labour-intensive unit dating from the 1930s to state-of-the-art computer-integrated manufacturing. The plant was designed to handle a large number of products (about 2500 variations). The new plant would look and feel very different from the existing plants operated by the organization. Altogether, covering the three shifts, a total of 128 new jobs were being created. The work force was to be selected from about 200 applicants from two existing refineries.

The company was concerned that the new recruits would not operate the system with sufficient flexibility, understanding and adaptation to the new working practices required – both by the new technology and by the culture of the new plant. Because of its commitment to optimum flexibility, the company decided to recruit the new employees into the plant as a group without initially allocating them to specific jobs, except for some unavoidable exceptions. In this way, it was thought, the new operators would be able to learn to adjust to the new environment without being blinkered by the past.

Design of the study

In order to define the attributes and qualities of the people who would be most suitable for working in the new plant, a JTR study was set up. The plant was still under construction, and no one had yet been recruited. Consequently, the study had to focus on experts who had the greatest knowledge of the jobs as they were likely to be. The management team had just been brought into existence, and therefore it was decided to focus most of the interviews on the departmental line managers. These included: the distribution manager, the administration and systems manager, the production manager, the engineering manager, the chief chemist, and the regional personnel manager. In addition to the management team, several members of the project team which was responsible for the design, construction and initial commissioning of the new plant were also interviewed. These were the project engineer, and specialists in filling lines, instrumentation, electrics, etc.

A secondary objective of the interviews was to gather sufficient information to attempt to cluster tasks and jobs into broad bands. The only data available in written form were a set of draft job descriptions that were of a highly speculative nature.

Data gathering

Altogether, 18 interviews of one and a half hours' duration were carried out. These focused on the jobs or clusters of tasks for which the manager or expert was responsible, but concentrated less on what people had to do in order to carry out tasks rather than on the *way* in which it was hoped the tasks would be carried out. The most suitable instrument to use for this purpose was judged to be the JLA (Job Learning Analysis). Using the structure provided by the JLA, the interviews focused on the extent to which the new tasks or jobs would require the operators to make decisions, memorize material by heart, prioritize, predict and anticipate, diagnose and solve problems, and adapt to new systems or ideas. Within this structure, the interviewers sought critical incidents by asking the interviewees to describe examples where they felt an operative would display desirable job behaviour, e.g. good anticipation, when carrying out a particular set of tasks, as well as provide examples of less desirable behaviour.

The interviews were open-ended, though they all followed a systematic structure. It was most important that the data-gathering did not become weighed down with too much detail, for fear of losing sight of attributes and characteristics that might be significant across wide bands of activity, or indeed the new plant as a whole. In conducting the interviews the aim was also to try and capture a concrete picture of what the new culture would be like in practical terms, i.e. the kind of specific behaviour that would represent the new culture.

	From	*To*
Organization of Work	Emphasis on Jobs	Emphasis on Tasks Activities/Roles
	Demarcation	Flexibility across activities
	Elaborate hierarchy	Flatter organization
	Self-contained functions	Interdependent functions
	Individuals in groups	Teamworking
Job Performance	Mainly physical manipulative work	Greater need for understanding and conceptual skills
	Specific/concrete things	More emphasis on ideas and principles
	Immediate feedback on performance	Remote, delayed feedback
	Localized consequences of action	Widespread consequences
	Knowledge of immediate environment	System-wide monitoring
Job Demands	Large groups	Dispersed teams
	Safety in numbers	Increased isolation/ vulnerability
	Close supervision	Increased autonomy/ self-monitoring
	Restricted decision-making	Devolved decision-making and responsibility
	A familiar learned environment	An unfamiliar learning environment
Problems	Steady/familiar	Dynamic/unfolding
	Proven technology	State-of-the-art technology (unproven?)
	Stability	Uncertainty
Values	Imposed from above "Sell what we make"	Shared/internalized "Make what the market needs"

Figure 5.6   *Characteristics of the new culture derived from the JLA/CI interviews.*

Results

The main results of the interviews fell into two broad categories. The first was a clearer definition of the new culture that was being created in the plant (summarized in Fig. 5.6). The results of the interviews were also used to formulate the selection criteria for the new centre. These came under five broad headings. They were:

Learning skills These included being open-minded and having an enquiring mind, seeking feedback on one's own performance and a desire to improve oneself, as well as being a ready and active learner who shows adaptability and versatility in the things she or he tries to learn.

Capacity to understand the system This involved the ability to see multiple viewpoints, avoiding tunnel vision, adopting a systematic approach, the ability to follow complex instructions, and be logical as well as have good convergent thinking skills. It also included the ability to visualize complex relationships.

Capacity for autonomy This included a tolerance of uncertainty, a readiness to take on and accept responsibility, to be able to make clear and effective decisions, to like solving problems for oneself, and the ability, where appropriate, to challenge authority or at the very least ask difficult questions to increase their confidence that they are doing the right thing.

Adapting to the new This included a readiness to accept and even *like* change. It also included tolerance of unfamiliarity and uncertainty, and taking an active interest in new ideas.

Teamworking This included the ability to remain independent within a group and yet work co-operatively with it; to have an affiliative disposition and yet not be dependent on the group.

Use of the results

To ensure that the applicants for the new plant would be assessed as fairly and as rigorously as possible, and that they would not be typecast into traditional roles because of work they had done in

91

the past, selection for the new plant was based primarily on the five core criteria. Formal assessment of strengths and weaknesses was made during the induction period, after which new recruits were allocated to appropriate functions and jobs. In order to facilitate this process, a Self-Assessment Questionnaire was devised in which the applicants were told at the beginning of each question what the new centre was looking for, and then asked to give examples, or information from their work history or their experience outside work that they felt would be relevant. No shortlisting took place as the number of applicants vis-à-vis the number of vacancies was relatively low. Accordingly, the Self-Assessment Questionnaire was primarily an aid to the interview.

The interview itself was structured round the five core selection criteria and a detailed interview plan was prepared; the new plant managers were trained in the use of the plan. It was specifically designed to elicit information relevant to the five-core criteria, in addition to other data concerning such matters as health, work record, etc.

Key points

(1) This study demonstrated a number of things, including that effective JTR analysis can take place even though there are no employees on which to base the analysis.

(2) The structure provided by the JLA and the interviewing technique embodied in Critical Incidents Technique were effective in eliciting less tangible, but none the less critically important, information that was relevant to the successful operation of the plant.

(3) The design of the Self-Assessment Questionnaire and the interview plan with associated guidance on interpretation of the data could not have been developed without the JTR analysis.

(4) Line managers as well as experts can be used effectively in a JTR analysis.

(5) JTR analysis can be used to define the attributes of organizational culture as well as define tasks and jobs.

CASE STUDY 3

Analysis of Driver Behaviour: The use of observation, critical incidents, PAQ, and repertory grid to analyse reasons for vehicle damage

Background

The Transport Division of a large corporation was concerned with the high level of damage to its vehicles – approximately 18% of its workshop time was devoted to accident repairs at a cost of around £2 million a year, which was well above the industry average. The drivers used a wide range of vehicles ranging from specialized handling equipment to public service vehicles and HGVs. One symptom giving cause for concern was that 50% of the accidents reported were of "unknown cause".

Management was convinced that improvements initially to the selection of drivers and subsequently to their training would significantly reduce accidents and vehicle damage. A JTR study was thus implemented in order to identify those areas in which drivers were most in need of training in order to reduce the accident/damage levels to vehicles.

Design of the study

The study began with brief periods of observation during which the drivers were accompanied and informally observed while they went about their work. Critical-incident interviews were included in order to identify good or effective driver behaviour as distinct from less effective and/or dangerous behaviour.

The PAQ was included as part of the study so as to ascertain whether the conditions under which the drivers do their work imposed exceptional demands on them – thus making their jobs atypical as far as motor transport drivers are concerned. Repertory grid interviews were also carried out in order to identify the constructs that drivers were using in approaching their work.

93

Data gathering

Observation was feasible on rare occasions only and a total of seven hours in a small range of vehicles was the maximum possible. Altogether, about 40 drivers out of a total of 120 were involved in individual interviews or group discussions. Critical-incident interviews, lasting up to two hours, were conducted with 18 drivers drawn from the three main departments within the transport division. These interviews focused on examples of particularly good or particularly poor driver behaviour. No one was identified by name but interviewees were encouraged to describe in some detail incidents that they had witnessed or knew about. On the basis of these interviews a list of driver behaviours was prepared, listing safe, effective driving on the one hand, and careless, irresponsible or even dangerous behaviour on the other.

PAQ interviews were conducted with six drivers. It was widely recognized that the drivers' working conditions were difficult, as they often drive in conditions of extreme traffic congestion and under considerable time pressure. In addition to the PAQ interviews, repertory-grid discussions were carried out with two groups of the 10 drivers. In these discussions, which lasted approximately two hours, the drivers were asked to compare and contrast critical elements using the repertory-grid method. They were given triads such as the following:

a safe PSV driver
a safe HGV driver
a duty supervisor

They were then asked to identify the two which were most alike and thus different from the third. Following group discussion, an underlying construct or dimension was identified, e.g., 'sticks to the regulations – does not stick to the regulations'. The group made a large number of these comparisons, using different elements in the triads, and 15 to 20 different constructs were elicited. Then the group as a whole went back over all the elements that had been used in the triads and decided whether, on balance, each element came at one end of the spectrum or the other.

When this process had been completed, the results were analysed by a statistical method known as cluster analysis (though in practice visual inspection alone, with some simple calculations, is often sufficient).

Results

The main result was that level of driver skill and the need for training did *not* appear to be the main factor in contributing to the high level of accidents and vehicle damage. Though they were important, there were a number of much more important factors in contributing to the overall level of accidents and damage: the design of the vehicles themselves, the environment in which they were driven, the management style, and the attitudes of the drivers themselves. The interaction of the management style (aloof, preoccupied, stressed) and the drivers' attitudes (alienated, frustrated, unsupervised) emerged as the main contributors to the high level of vehicle damage and accidents.

The JTR analysis also revealed an obsession with haste, a result of what the drivers saw as a management requirement that they should carry out their duties as fast as possible. This obsession was exacerbated by the supervisors, who were themselves under considerable pressure. When this was combined with the virtually total absence of accountability for vehicles and equipment and the development of rivalries and conflicts between different sections and shifts, a 'vehicle bashing culture' developed.

In addition, the study revealed that the drivers worked under very stressful conditions caused by time pressure, noise, congestion, frustrations, etc. Individual factors (e.g. variations in individual driving skill) explained *some* of the damage that was being done but by no means all of it.

Use of the results

Since individual driver skill was not the main factor contributing to damage of vehicles and equipment, training would not immediately help reduce the problem. A vicious circle had developed, which had to be broken. The 'vehicle bashing culture' was being sustained partly by a system of low accountability for vehicles, an obsession with haste, and other factors such as habitual rule-breaking, rivalry, conflict and a general feeling of alienation.

As a result, it was necessary to introduce significant organizational and management change, including policy clarification, before any new driver training or safety education. A working party was set up to investigate further and bring about the necessary changes.

95

Key points

(1) This study demonstrates the value of the JTR approach over traditional job analysis. A conventional job analysis study would have focused on trying to identify which aspects of driver skill were associated with accident or damage to vehicles. Though this was recognized to be an important ingredient, however, the wider framework of the JTR approach permitted interpretation and analysis of the wider cultural and organizational issues which might be at the root of the problem.

(2) The study also demonstrates how different data-gathering techniques can be combined to form a more complete picture.

(3) Relatively small demands of driver time and resources were necessary to analyse a complex organizational problem.

(4) Although the repertory-grid data analysis was subjected to computer-based statistical analysis, with hindsight this was judged to be unnecessary.

CASE STUDY 4

Analysis and Comparison of Two Jobs: Use of job components inventory, critical incidents and repertory grid in a cigarette factory

Background

A cigarette manufacturer was embarking on a major reorganization of the way work was carried out. There were a number of different types of cigarette-making machines, which produced cigarettes at rates of between 2,500 and 7,500 per minute. The traditional way of working was to have a number of machine minders and one machine mechanic on each machine. The minder's primary role was to feed the machine with the appropriate materials and maintain quality. The mechanic's primary role was to repair the machine when it broke down. Speed was of the essence: every minute the machine was down meant a loss of at least 2,500 cigarettes. Reorganization was going to involve a reduction in the numbers of people working on each machine, as it had been decided that the roles of machine minder and machine mechanic would be combined into a new post of "minder/mechanic". The initial decision was to turn all the mechanics into minder/mechanics, since the training for a minder could be measured in terms of weeks whereas a mechanic's apprenticeship took approximately three years. This proposal, therefore, would have led to the removal of many (if not all) of the minders from the organization; the difficulty was that they were women, while all the mechanics were men, which meant that a whole tier of women workers would have been eliminated at a stroke.

It was decided to undertake a JTR analysis to discover whether it would be possible to train a minder in the mechanics' skills in a reasonably short period of time, and, if this was possible, to recommend a selection procedure which identified the minders who had the appropriate skills to become minder/mechanics. Finally, if it was feasible to train minders to become mechanics, the organization wanted to have a clear idea of where the skill gaps were.

Design of the study

The primary aim of the study was to make a comparison between the jobs of a minder and a mechanic, so both jobs were analysed separately and the results compared. The techniques which were used included the observation interview, the Job Components Inventory, the Critical Incidents Technique and the Repertory Grid.

The machines involved are very large and complicated, so before any interviews could be undertaken it was necessary for the analysts to observe them at work. Due to the noise from the machines and the speed at which the minders worked, it was not possible to ask questions as they were carrying out their work. Once the observations had been completed, therefore, the minders and the analysts went into a quieter room for an informal interview. (The basic observation period, incidentally, also provided the analysts with an introduction to the technical terms used.)

In order to make direct and concrete comparisons between the two jobs, it was necessary to employ a technique which provided quantifiable data. Given the nature of the work that was being carried out (i.e. semi-skilled/skilled, involving the use of tools and equipment), it was felt that the Job Components Inventory (JCI) would provide the most detailed and comprehensive information.

The JCI does indeed provide a very good description of the observable aspects of jobs, but it is far weaker for the mental processes involved which, it was recognized, could be critical components in the way the work was performed. The main aim of the mechanic's job, for example, was to find faults occurring in the machine, to analyse problems, and to produce solutions which got the machine working again as quickly as possible. To enable these critical mental processes to be identified, the Critical Incidents Technique and the Repertory Grid were adopted as suitable and flexible enough to be applied to both jobs.

Data gathering

A wide range of people were interviewed by using the different techniques. For example, observation and JCI interviews were carried out directly with the co-operation and assistance of minders and mechanics; Critical Incidents interviews with minders, mechanics and supervisors; Repertory Grid interviews with the supervisors.

98

The whole process was carried out over a period of five days by two analysts. Furthermore, a Group Critical Incidents exercise for both minders and mechanics was carried out. Of all the techniques used, this was probably the least successful. There was a great deal of anxiety and tension within the company about re-organization and redundancies, and this anxiety was felt particularly keenly by the minders. In the group discussion, therefore, these frustrations and anxieties came to the fore, as might have been expected.

MINDER	MECHANIC
Pen	Fila Gauge
Knives	Thermometer
Cleaning Fluids	Pressure Gauge
Brushes	Mallet
Bellows	Spanners
	Allen Keys
	Screwdrivers
	Files
	Emery Cloth
	Sharpening Stones
	Grinder
	Vices
	Pliers
	Tweezers
	Hand-saw
	Snips
	Knives
	Chisels
	Scissors
	Oil
	Glue
	White Spirit
	Abrasive Paper
	Detergents
	Brushes
	Aerosols
	Brushes, Brooms
	Vacuums
	Cloths, Rags, Mops
	Filters
	Lifts
	Telephone

Figure 5.7 *Tools list, based on JCI analysis*

Results

When the jobs of machine minder and mechanic were compared using the JCI, the biggest differences were found in the areas of the tools used and the mathematical skills required. It can be seen in Figure 5.7, for example, that minders used very few tools and little equipment, compared with the mechanics.

With this information available, it was possible to identify the skills gaps. Ability to use the range of tools currently employed by mechanics was seen as essential for anyone in the minder/ mechanic post. People not familiar with such tools or equipment obviously required training. It was estimated, however, that such training would not take long or be particularly complex because the tools (and the tasks for which they were used) were reasonably simple.

		MINDER	MECHANIC
E6	Responsibility for injury or death	•	•
E7	Responsibility for damage to tools and equipment	•	•
E8	Responsibility for lost time	•	•
E1	Responsibility about work order	•	•
E2	Deciding about methods or procedures	•	•
E3	Deciding about tools and materials	•	•
E4	Deciding what to do if things go wrong	•	•
E5	Deciding about standards	•	•
E9	Responsibility for things needing special precautions		•

Figure 5.8   *Decision-making and responsibility*

Figure 5.8 shows the results obtained in the decision-making and responsibilities category of the JCI. It can be seen that minders and mechanics share the same skills in these areas. The biggest difference is that mechanics have more discretion in the decisions they make (for example in selecting priorities, determining which tools to use), whereas minders are more likely to follow set

100

procedures. However, the skills gap in this case was not very great because the minders demonstrated the relevant skills in their current work, although they might need training in how to determine priorities.

Analysis of the Critical Incidents and Repertory Grid data revealed the key skills which good minders and mechanics must have. These skills are summarized in Figure 5.9; it is obvious that both classes of worker require many of the same characteristics. For example, with the appreciation of business needs, miners must be interested in production targets; they need to have an awareness of the importance of production and the implications for the business generally if the machine is down for long periods. Mechanics, on the other hand, have to assess the seriousness of faults and make decisions about whether a machine should be knocked off or not. A good mechanic would keep the machine running for as long as possible and repair minor faults at weekends, so they too were clearly aware of the importance of keeping the machines running.

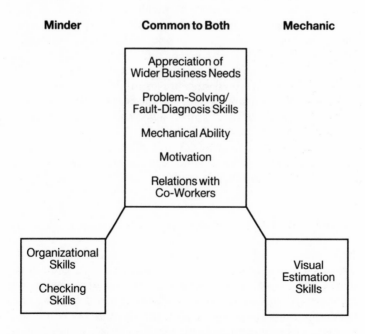

Figure 5.9 *Critical Skills required of a Minder and a Mechanic*

The skills gap in this case was that people selected for the minder/mechanic post would have to be taught what constitutes a serious problem, and which problems can safely be left for a while. It was felt to be possible, however, to identify general principles which apply to many if not all machines, and to give further training on specific machines.

For problem-solving and fault-diagnosis, minders must be alert and aware of what is happening in all parts of the machine. Good minders remain vigilant, hoping to identify and deal with any fault before it becomes too problematic; they thus avoid knocking the machine off, if it is at all possible. They are also systematic in locating and identifying the source.

Mechanics had to identify the cause of a fault from a far wider range of possibilities, but they too had to be systematic in their problem-solving. Again the skills gap was in the level rather than the type of skill.

All of the other critical aspects of the work of the two groups were analysed in this way, and the skill gaps identified. The analysis revealed that skill gaps were not only present for the minders – there were some areas where the mechanics might need special training. The minders had a greater responsibility for supervising others and ensuring that crews worked efficiently. This entailed watching if materials were running out, organizing break periods, recognizing when more assistance was needed, deciding which task should be performed first (for example on a dual-operated machine). All these were aspects of the work which would have been unfamiliar to mechanics, who had always worked in isolation and not as members of a team.

Checking skills were another area where the mechanics had little experience. (Minders were responsible for quality, which meant examining the cigarettes for faults.)

Use of the results

The results indicated that there was a considerable overlap in the qualities needed by minders and mechanics. A good minder already had to possess many of the qualities of a good minder/mechanic. As a result of this, a selection procedure was introduced which was designed to identify the minders who had the potential to become minder/mechanics. This consisted of aptitude tests and an evidence-based interview checklist (which included questions that interviewers could ask the candidates and an outline of the sort of evidence which would count in the candidate's favour, and against him or her).

Key points

(1) The JTR analysis indicated that the assumptions about the level of training required to enable a minder to become a minder/mechanic were not borne out by the evidence. There was not a great difference in skill levels between the minder's and mechanic's job; the training required would not be too expensive for the organization to consider. Good minders already possessed many of the skills required of a minder/mechanic, albeit at a lower level.

(2) Although the JTR analysis was undertaken for a selection and training objective, the method of comparing two jobs has obvious applications in other areas, particularly job evaluation.

(3) Questionnaire methods, although very useful in providing quantified information (particularly about the content of the work), tend to miss out on the mental processes involved. In this case, the Critical Incidents Technique and the Repertory Grid gave a good indication of the mental skills required, which the JCI could not have provided.

CASE STUDY 5

JTR Analysis and Fair Selection: Clerical staff in a commercial bank

Background

The bank recruits a large number of clerical staff every year, which gives rise to the problem of shortlisting on a fair basis, ensuring that no race or sex discrimination occurs. A JTR analysis was conducted in order to identify the skill areas required in the clerical grades, so that the questions on the application form could direct candidates' attention to providing information in these areas. Another objective of the project was to design a recruitment guide for selectors incorporating a detailed person specification of the type of candidate needed.

Design of the study

Although all entrants come in at the first clerical grade, the bank wanted people who would be able to progress to at least the third grade. The three grades were therefore analysed to determine the similarities in skills and abilities required. These core attributes could then be listed in the recruitment guide. The first task was to select for analysis certain jobs from the wide range which were currently performed. By means of the job descriptions, a sample of 16 jobs were identified as representative. The techniques used to analyse the jobs included:

(1) Observations. These were carried out so that the analysts could familiarize themselves with the environment and the range of jobs performed by the new entrants.

(2) PAQ. This particular technique enabled a quantitative comparison to be made between the different types of jobs. It also enabled the analysts to obtain a very broad-brush general view of the work.

(3) Individual and group critical incident interviews. The critical incident technique was the main method used, since it enabled the analysts to identify the critical skills and abilities which are required of new entrants to the bank.

104

The bank is divided into a number of regional units and it was felt to be important that the job analysis covered as many of the regions as was practicable. This was for two reasons:

(1) In order to identify whether there were differences in the way the jobs were being performed in different regions.

(2) In order to obtain the cooperation of the managers in the different regions, so that they were involved in the process and would thus feel more committed to any new recruitment guidelines which were produced.

Data gathering

Approximately 60 people were seen altogether: jobholders in each of the clerical grades and supervisors in the fourth and higher grades. Supervisory staff were used particularly in the group critical incident discussions. Interviews and analysis were carried out in a number of different regions and the data gathering itself took approximately 3 months.

Results

As part of the analysis of the PAQ data, a cluster analysis was carried out. This indicated that there were no major differences between the way jobs were performed in the different regions. It also indicated that, although there were some differences in the types of skills required in the different jobs, these were often not significant. It was therefore possible, using the PAQ results in combination with the critical incident information, to define quite clearly the skills needed for a wide range of jobs in the first three clerical grades.

Three main skills areas were identified:

(1) People skills
(2) Office skills
(3) Job demands.

People skills included things such as being able to provide an excellent service, remaining calm and controlled under pressure or in frustrating circumstances, possessing persuasive/selling skills (which involves linking customers' requirements with the bank's services and handling people confidently, and preferring to work in the company of others).

Office skills covered such things as accuracy in keeping records and checking documentation. Furthermore, jobholders had to be organized and systematic enough to deal with several different types of documentation. They had to know where to obtain information when required and how to keep records in order and up-to-date. They had to adopt or develop systems to organize the job and meet deadlines.

Jobholders also had to be able to follow procedures laid down by the bank, to adhere to them despite pressures from customers and other sources, and to accept this as an essential part of the job. Basic numeracy skills were required – addition, subtraction, multiplication and division, using and understanding percentages and fractions – but not high levels of mathematical ability. The same applied to basic literacy skills, like being able to complete a wide variety of standard forms and letters and to read job instructions, manuals and memos.

Job demands included versatility in handling a variety of different tasks and equipment with little formal instruction. Jobholders had to be able to adapt quickly to changes in working practices and procedures while maintaining the quality of their work. They also had to be able to learn without close supervision or formal training.

Use of the results

Once the skills had been identified and defined it was a straightforward matter to convert this information into a recruitment guide for selectors. The guide indicated the skills required and provided detailed definitions of what each skill area meant. It gave examples of occasions when each type of skill was needed.

The critical incident technique proved extremely valuable both in identifying skills and abilities and in providing specific examples of occasions when a particular skill was required. This type of information added a bit of colour to the recruitment guide and also provided a far more concrete means of determining the level of skill employed in any particular job.

The next step was to use the person specification as a guide for determining the design of the application form. This was done in close collaboration with staff from the personnel department of the bank. In the following areas, it was decided that more information from the candidates would be useful:

(1) Dealing with other people
(2) Following set procedures, completing forms, working accurately, etc.
(3) Learning new skills
(4) Analysing information, organizing work, etc.
(5) Supervising other people.

Candidates were told on the application form that they should provide *any* experience relevant to each of these categories, including school and education, paid or unpaid work, family life and leisure interests. This was done because it was felt that some people, in particular women, may have gained a lot of relevant experience in the home which is often not considered at all. There were also a series of questions on the back of the application form designed to produce more specific information on some of the relevant areas.

In order to finalize the process, a document was produced for recruiters, indicating how the application form should be used and the type of information they should be looking for. Furthermore, a shortlisting form was designed so that recruiters could indicate quickly the areas in which an applicant had experience and whether or not he or she should be shortlisted.

Key points

(1) JTR analysis can be used to produce a selection procedure which is systematic and standardized and which assesses the skills relevant to the performance of a particular job. The case study also indicates the usefulness of the critical incidents technique in identifying key skills and abilities for jobs so that person specifications can be developed.

(2) The critical incidents technique can be used to identify the type of information and experience which are in a candidate's favour and those which are not. Although the PAQ provides a broad-brush picture of a job, it would not be suitable for analysis at such a thorough level.

(3) JTR analysis is very appropriate for producing fairer selection procedures which comply with the codes of practice of both the Commission for Racial Equality and the Equal Opportunities Commission. If followed, the new procedures should certainly reduce the possibility of unfair discrimination.

6
Mini Case Studies

MINI CASE STUDY 1

Repertory Technique to Design Job Appraisal Forms

This particular case study involved the management services division of a manufacturing organization. At one level were the computer programmers and systems analysts; above them were senior analysts and project leaders. The problem was twofold: the management were not happy about the selection of new recruits; and there was some dissatisfaction about the way in which senior systems analysts and project leaders were appointed. In neither case had there been any attempt to identify clearly the skills and abilities required. In order to improve the selection process, tests were to be introduced, along with a concurrent validation study.

The JTR analysis was used to design a job performance appraisal form, to be completed by supervisors.

The JTR analysis itself was relatively small-scale and took only a few days to complete; the repertory grid technique was the main method used. To analyse the programmers' and systems analysts' jobs, their supervisors (i.e. senior analysts and project leaders) were interviewed. For the senior analysts and project leaders, senior management were interviewed.

The repertory grid was considered to be sufficient because of the wealth of information gathered from the people interviewed. Laddering was used to obtain concrete and detailed descriptions of behaviour which distinguished between good and less good job performance. These job behaviours were then written on to separate cards and categorized into a number of different skills and abilities: analytical abilities, people skills, etc. For each category of abilities, it was possible to draw up a number of behaviourally anchored rating scales, which were combined to produce a form. An example is given in Figure 6.1. The job performance appraisal form was given to the supervisors, who then assessed their subordinates. The ratings from the forms were correlated with the test scores, and the tests which had a strong statistical relationship with job performance were used as part of the new selection procedure.

I *Analytical Ability*

A1 Probes in depth before reaching a solution

Top 5%
programmers   Average   Bottom 5%
                                                          programmers

A2 Adopts a structured, methodical approach

Top 5%
programmers   Average   Bottom 5%
                                                          programmers

A3 Ability to come up with new concepts for system design

Top 5%
programmers   Average   Bottom 5%
                                                          programmers

A4 Quickly becomes expert when dealing
with new technology or systems

Top 5%
programmers   Average   Bottom 5%
                                                          programmers

A5 Ability to focus on the key issues of a problem

Top 5%
programmers   Average   Bottom 5%
                                                          programmers

A6 Ability to find solutions to problems unaided

Top 5%
programmers   Average   Bottom 5%
                                                          programmers

A7 Ability to use procedures intelligently

Top 5%
programmers   Average   Bottom 5%
                                                          programmers

II *Practical Application*

P1 Systems set up do not need adjusting

Top 5%
programmers   Average   Bottom 5%
                                                          programmers

P2 Able to satisfactorily combine technical
and business viewpoints

Top 5%
programmers   Average   Bottom 5%
                                                          programmers

Figure 6.1 *Examples of rating scales for an appraisal form*

The repertory grid data were also used to produce interview checklists which indicated, for each ability area, the type of questions which could be asked and the type of evidence which would count for or against the candidate.

This particular example indicated the power of the Repertory Grid technique when used with people who approach tasks very analytically and are able to ladder in a detailed and concrete way.

MINI CASE STUDY 2

Using the JLA to Evaluate Current Training Provision

The Sales and Customer Services Training Division of a major airline was carrying out a thorough review of the content and presentation of the training material which it prepares and distributes to travel agency staff. Training is provided by college lecturers, airline instructors, and by means of self-study through correspondence. A group of instructors were trained in the use of the JLA in a two-day workshop. They then carried out JLA interviews, focusing specifically on fares and ticketing in five different travel agents across the country. When the interviews had been completed, the results were analysed by the whole group. They identified a need to encourage learners to think through the procedures they were being taught, rather than just following them in a passive and mechanical way. For example, analysis revealed that trainees were not encouraged to ask questions such as: 'Why is travel geography important? What could go wrong if I did not know my travel geography? What do I need to know about travel geography? How can I best learn these things?'

Three other areas were judged to be important: the learning of new ideas and systems; checking and assessing; and predicting and anticipating. It was preferable, the instructors concluded, to teach students the basic principles of air fares and ticketing so they could cope with the wide variations in details and particulars. It was also judged to be more appropriate to teach trainees how to keep themselves up-to-date with developments rather than getting them to memorize particular procedures solely for the certificating exam.

Under the heading of "checking and assessing", it was concluded that existing material concentrated on the basics, but did not teach the trainee how to assess the benefits of one type of fare against another, or different fares for different types of holiday. There was a need for new training material to develop this kind of learning. (Previously, most people had learned by "sitting by Nellie", or through complaints from dissatisfied customers.)

As a result of the study, checking, assessing and evaluating were also seen to be important skills of the job, which could be practised and developed by being built into the training programme.

112

With regard to predicting and anticipating (particularly important in the context of anticipating customer problems), it was concluded that training did not develop these skills.

As a result of the JLA interviews, a number of new training exercises were designed to develop understanding, anticipation and evaluation in the trainees. For example, ticket-issuing had frequently been taught as a simple *procedure*, which trainees attempted to memorize without comprehending the reasons for doing things. In order to develop appropriate strategies, the instructor introduced questioning demonstrations, announcing that he or she was going to demonstrate ticket-issuing for a complex itinerary, and inviting trainees to ask as many questions as they liked. The instructor only gave information in response to questions and the trainees were thus encouraged to ask about purposes, problems, comparisons with other procedures, and how to check whether they had carried out something correctly.

MINI CASE STUDY 3

Using JTR Analysis to Group Brewery Production Jobs

A large brewery wished to recruit new employees into a bulk packaging plant which was nearing completion. High-speed filling lines were being introduced, which required shifts of fifteen people to work on each line. Although the technology was not much more advanced than that used elsewhere in the brewery, the lines were considerably faster.

The objectives of the study were to identify relevant job-related criteria, and to draft employee specifications for each job or group of jobs which could be used in the selection process. Jobs had to be separated into broad bands since the brewery wanted to recruit people into a group rather than a specific job. Accordingly, each employee had to be capable of doing *all* the jobs within the group.

A variety of data-gathering methods were used. About 30 to 45 minutes were spent observing and questioning an experienced worker in another packaging plant of the brewery, where similar, though not identical, lines had already been introduced. The Job Components Inventory was used for each of the fifteen jobs since it is ideal for identifying in great detail the kinds of tools, levels of arithmetical reasoning, etc. that are involved in a job. In addition, the Position Analysis Questionnaire was used, because it is the only technique currently available which can scale a particular job against all other jobs by reference to its norm base. In this way, direct comparison was possible between jobs in terms of the skill, effort and other demands made on the individual. A cluster analysis of the PAQ data could then determine whether the jobs could be meaningfully grouped.

In addition, the more complex jobs were subjected to critical incident interviews with supervisors. The interviewer asked the supervisor for descriptions of real job behaviour they had witnessed which they felt was particularly good, and descriptions of behaviour they felt was less effective or where avoidable mistakes were made. Altogether, twelve PAQ interviews and twelve critical incident interviews were conducted; together with the eight JCI interviews, this made a total of 32 interviews. Five distinct groups of jobs were identified. These were:

(1) Quality controller.
(2) Pasteurizer, Cleaning In Place, and Cleaner.

(3) Forklift truck driver; Stock control.
(4) Palletizer, Depalletizer, Labeller, Capsuler, Decant operator.
(5) Decoder.

For each group of jobs, a person specification was developed and the critical features were identified; altogether, 22 specific skills and abilities were identified for the jobs, though the relevant number for a group of jobs ranged from 5 up to a maximum of 13.

The study showed that a common set of job behaviours can be developed, from which the requirements for specific jobs can be selected. The study also demonstrated the usefulness of the JCI in preparing job descriptions, which compensated for the lack of detailed information of that kind obtained from the PAQ.

MINI CASE STUDY 4

Identifying Selection Criteria in an Employment Agency

A leading employment agency was concerned that they might not be attracting and selecting the right kind of people to act as interviewers. Selections had been made according to the subjective perceptions of existing managers and proper criteria had never been defined. A study was therefore set up to identify the characteristics of successful interviewers.

Critical incident interviews lasting up to two hours were carried out with nine existing interviewers, nine branch managers, six area controllers; there were also two group discussions to elicit critical incidents with a further sixteen managers. Interviews were conducted with four senior managers, and the PAQ used. The results indicated that eight broad criteria were relevant:

- Information-processing skills;

- Interpersonal skills;

- Planning and organizing;

- Self-control;

- Task/team orientation;

- Memory and attention;

- Service orientation;

- Oral skills.

In the light of these findings, a structured evidence-based interview procedure was developed to focus specifically on the eight criteria identified, and particular aptitude tests were recommended. Before accepting the recommendations, it was agreed that the criteria should be tested and evaluated along with the tests.

A behaviourally anchored performance rating scale was developed around the eight criteria. An example of the scale for information-processing skills is given below:

116

Good	Poor
Likes to weigh up relevant pros and cons before reaching a conclusion.	Tends to rely on assumptions; less good at interpreting information available; does not check and follow up information received.

The rating form covered the eight criteria identified in the JTR study, plus two further ratings for overall performance and its "general direction" (improvement or decline). A random sample of experienced interviewers were rated by both their immediate line managers and their division directors. In addition, objective data on revenue generated by each individual over a specified period, and the number of months they were above their target, were also gathered. In this way, the objective measures of performance could be related to the managers' ratings. In addition, the interviewers were tested on the recommended aptitude tests, to ascertain whether the tests would predict the objective measures of their job performance, the managers' evaluations or both.

The analysis revealed that the recommended tests did *not* correlate with either of the objective measures of job performance. However, the ratings on the eight criteria were consistently and significantly related to the objective measures, as well as to the subjective measures of overall job performance.

In the light of the analysis, the employer agreed to adopt the eight criteria as formal selection standards and to use them as the basis for training and development. In due course, the rating form was adapted for use in performance appraisal.

7
A Do-it-yourself JTR Method

This chapter offers a structured JTR analysis interview covering a broad range of tasks and duties performed at work and also provides analysts with a series of probing questions which can be used to elicit more information from a jobholder. The technique itself is designed to be easy to use with very little training and to provide a good broad-brush picture of a job in a relatively short space of time. It is not intended to replace any of the more sophisticated JTR techniques but it recognizes that line managers and others involved in the recruitment and selection process often lack the skills or time to carry out a complex analysis. It enables recruiters and line managers to obtain information:

(1) in a quick, efficient way
(2) which provides a relatively detailed understanding of the way the job is being performed and
(3) gives an indication of the types of skills and abilities which are required to perform it.

Despite its limitations, it has been used successfully in a number of organizations, for example to analyse the job of a finance director in an international airport.

USING THE STRUCTURED JOB ANALYSIS INTERVIEW

The structure for the interview is as follows:

1. Place in the organization

The job is placed in relation to others in the organization.

2. Main objective

The overall objective or aim of the job should be established in a few brief sentences which are neither too complex nor too bland. Care and attention at this stage pays dividends, since it provides a point of reference for the rest of the interview.

3. Main duties and activities

The main objective of the job can then be broken down into more detailed subordinate operations. You should rate the main duty for its importance to the job and the amount of time spent performing it. The following rating scales should be used:

Importance to the job:

4 Extremely important
3 Highly important
2 Moderately important
1 Unimportant

In using this scale, it is worthwhile considering the consequences of an error in any of the duties (i.e. what would happen if a particular task was not carried out at all, or was carried out badly?).

Amount of time:

4 Very substantial - over 66% of the time
3 Considerable - between 33% and 66% of the time
2 Moderate - between 10% and 33% of the time
1 Very little - less than 10% of the time

This particular scale sometimes causes a little difficulty for people being interviewed since they may not be able to determine the amount of time spent on a particular activity very precisely. This does not matter, as the analyst only really needs a rough guide.

4. Decision-making and responsibilities

This examines questions such as the amount of supervision received; numbers of people supervised; types of decision made; types of tools/equipment/machines used; etc.

5. Contact with others

The information obtained here concentrates on the types of people the jobholder comes into contact with; in what ways; how often; and for what reasons.

6. Physical environment

The type of place in which the work is conducted:

In asking these questions, you should attempt to obtain as much information as possible – the more information you have, the greater the chances of drawing up job descriptions and person specifications which are accurate. Responses to the questions should be recorded on the response sheets (see pages 122 and 123).

PREPARING FOR A STRUCTURED JOB ANALYSIS INTERVIEW

There are a number of considerations which the analyst must bear in mind before the interview.

1. Be familiar with the material

The analyst must make sure that she/he is familiar with the interview material, which means understanding the questions, how to record the answers, and how to interpret the results.

2. Be familiar with the job

Although a lot of detailed information will be obtained using the questionnaire, it is important that analysts have an initial overview of the job. If they are not familiar with the job, they should, at the very least, look at the job descriptions. Ideally, jobholders should also be observed at work.

3. Choosing the right people to interview

The people chosen for interview should be good at their work and have at least one year's experience. If the analyst is not familiar with jobholders' work performance, assistance will be required from the supervisors. Ideally, at least two people should be interviewed for each job.

4. Introducing the interview

Jobholders to be interviewed will sometimes have misgivings

about the objectives of the interview. Some might think it is a form of performance appraisal, others mistake it for job evaluation. For the interview to be effective, these misapprehensions must be dispelled. The introduction to the interview, therefore, should make its purpose clear, and the analyst should stress that it is not a performance appraisal, a test or a personality questionnaire.

One should always remember that although it is of a very specific kind, a job analysis interview is an interview, so all the principles of good interview technique apply.

A model introduction is given in Figure 7.1. (It is assumed that the analyst has already introduced him/herself to the jobholder.)

'As you know, a vacancy has occurred for a job at the same grade as yours and we are about to start the recruitment process. Obviously, we want to make sure that the person we appoint has the skills which are needed to do the job. This interview is one of the ways in which we hope to gain a clearer picture of what the job involves. I will be interviewing you with this job analysis questionnaire, which is used to find out what you see as the main aim of your job. Then I will ask you to state the main activities in your work. After that, I will take each activity in turn and discuss them in more detail.

'In order to remember your answers, I will be taking brief notes. The interview will last approximately one and a half hours. I should stress that I am not assessing your job performance, nor is this a test of any sort. Furthermore, there are no right or wrong answers. All the information you give me is absolutely confidential. Before we begin, have you any questions you would like to ask?'

Figure 7.1 *Example of an introduction to a job analysis interview*

5. Recording the answers

Answers to the questions should be recorded on the Job Analysis Response Sheets. Copies of these are given in Figures 7.2 and 7.3; when conducting a job analysis interview, you should prepare a supply in advance and write in the boxes the number of each question asked. The checklist of possible questions is presented below.

121

JOB TITLE: DEPARTMENT:

JOBS ABOVE:

JOBS BELOW:

MAIN OBJECTIVE:

MAIN DUTIES	Importance to the Job	Amount of Time

Figure 7.2 *Job analysis response sheets*

ITEM
NUMBER

☐ _____
_____
_____
_____
_____
_____
_____

☐ _____
_____
_____
_____
_____
_____
_____

☐ _____
_____
_____
_____
_____
_____
_____

Figure 7.3 *Job analysis response sheets (continued)*

123

STRUCTURED JOB ANALYSIS INTERVIEW

Place in the organization

1 What is your job title?
2 What department do you work in?
3 What jobs are immediately above yours?
4 What jobs are immediately below yours?

Main objective

5 What do you see as the main objective of your job?

Main duties

6 (a) What are your main duties/activities?
　 (b) How important are each of these to your work?
　 (c) What proportion of your time do you spend on each of these duties?

Duties and responsibilities

7 (a) What tools and equipment do you use?
　 (b) What do you use each of them for?
　 (c) How important are they to your work?
　 (d) How often do you use them?

8 (a) What aspects of your work require physical effort, i.e. carrying, pushing, pulling?
　 (b) What do you have to do?
　 (c) What sort of weight/force/pressure is involved?
　 (d) How often do you have to do this?

9 (a) What written materials do you use as sources of information, e.g. notes, reports, articles, etc?
　 (b) What do you use them for?
　 (c) How important are they to your work?
　 (d) How often do you use them?

10 (a) What writing do you do, e.g. reports, letters, memos?
　 (b) Who do you generally write to?
　 (c) Generally, what is the content of the written work?
　 (d) How do you decide what you have to write?
　 (e) How often do you have to write things?

11 (a) What materials do you use involving figures, tables of numbers, etc?
   (b) What do you use them for?
   (c) How important are they to your work?
   (d) How often do you use them?

12 (a) What figure work/calculations do you have to do?
   (b) What do you have to do it for?
   (c) What is the highest level of arithmetic you require (e.g. working with decimals and fractions, algebra, etc)?
   (d) How often do you work with figures?

13 (a) Do you use graphs, pictures or pictorial materials in your work?
   (b) What do you use them for?
   (c) How important are they?
   (d) How often do you use them?

14 (a) Do you ever have to produce maps/charts/diagrams, etc?
   (b) For what reasons?
   (c) How often do you do this?

15 (a) Which aspects of your work, if any, require you to work accurately?
   (b) What would the consequences be if you were not accurate in those areas?

16 (a) What other sources of information do you use in your work?
   (b) For what reason?
   (c) How important are they?

17 (a) Are professional qualifications required for this job?
   (b) What level of education is needed to be able to perform this work?

18 (a) Is previous experience required to perform this job?
   (b) If yes, what sort of experience is required? Be as specific as you can.
   (c) Why do you think that?
   (d) What is the minimum amount of time in which a person could have obtained such experience?

19 (a) How much supervision do you receive?
   (b) How much contact do you have with your supervisor?

(c) How does your supervisor know if your work is up to standard?

20 (a) How many people do you supervise?
     (b) What does that involve?

21 (a) How do you decide the order in which to carry out your work? (i.e. is it predetermined or are you free to set your own priorities?)

22 (a) What planning or organizing do you have to do?
     (b) What do you have to do it for?
     (c) How important is it to your work?
     (d) How often do you have to do it?

23 (a) How responsible are you for the safety of others?
     (b) What does this involve?
     (c) How important is this?

24 (a) What sorts of assets, material, money are you directly responsible for?
     (b) What does this involve?
     (c) How important is this?

Contact with others

25 (a) What people do you come into contact with in the organization?
     (b) For what reason?
     (c) How important is contact with each of these people?
     (d) How often do you come into contact with each of these people?

26 (a) What people from outside the organization do you come into contact with?
     (b) For what reason?
     (c) How important is contact with each of these people?
     (d) How often do you come into contact with each of these people?

27 (a) Is there any negotiating/interviewing/training/public speaking involved?
     (b) For what reason?
     (c) What does it involve?
     (d) How important is it?
     (e) How often do you have to do it?

28 (a) What are the major forms of contact (e.g. personal contact, telephone, letters, memos, etc)?
    (b) How important are these forms of contact?
    (c) How often do you use them?

Physical environment

29 (a) Is the majority of your work indoors or outdoors?
    (b) What proportion of time is spent indoors/outdoors?

30 (a) How many people do you work with most of the time?

31 (a) What are the physical conditions like (e.g. light, heat, space, etc)?

32 (a) To what extent do routines and procedures have to be followed?
    (b) For which activities?
    (c) How much time do you spend working under such routines and procedures?

33 (a) What are the prospects for future development?

8
Job, Task and Role Analysis: The Future

Since the 1970s, the number of developed and packaged techniques for analysing jobs, tasks and roles has grown rapidly. Six clear trends can be detected.

(1) Computer-based systems

Increasingly, computer-based techniques are being developed. The most elaborate example is the PAQ, which involves the comparison of ratings for an existing job with the average ratings of a highly representative sample of all the jobs in the economy. In addition, the PAQ computing services can calculate job evaluation points, carry out cluster analysis, group jobs, make test recommendations, and print lists of attributes that are associated with jobs defined in a particular way. It can even print out standardized job description pages.

(2) Computer-assisted systems

In addition to the complete PAQ package, computer-assisted systems like the WPSS will probably be of increasing importance in the future. Since they provide a suite of computer programmes for the analysis and presentation of results or large numbers of ratings, individual employers can develop their own highly specialized and job-specific checklists. In this way, they get the computing and analytical power of a standardized system with none of the disadvantages of a general-purpose checklist.

(3) More emphasis on processes

The majority of formal job analysis techniques (such as the Hierarchical Task Analysis, Job Components Inventory and Functional Job Analysis) place most, if not all, of their emphasis on describing the tasks and activities involved in a job. With the increasing introduction of new technology and changes in working practices, there will be much more emphasis on developing flexibility, autonomy and more generalizable attributes, as

128

opposed to the specific components of particular jobs. There will also be much more emphasis on jobholders' understanding and conceptual (rather than physical) skills. Consequently, there is likely to be increased demand for JTR analysis methods which assess processes rather than job content (such as the JLA and Job Element Examinings).

(4) Complete systems

The PAQ is the most elaborate complete system of JTR analysis. A standardized questionnaire is used as the basis for computing norm-based profiles or job evaluation comparisons; its many other applications range from human resource planning to career and vocational guidance. Considerable computing power is required to set up such a system, since it is based on a very large data bank supported by an extensive suite of programs. It also takes a considerable amount of time to develop a database which is sufficiently large so as to be representative of large sections of the economy. Nonetheless, given the success and wide-ranging applications of the PAQ, it is highly likely that other systems will be developed.

(5) Synthetic validity

Research in Britain and the United States from the 1960s onwards has revealed the insurmountable practical difficulties of conducting textbook validation studies which could justify the use of pencil and paper tests and other selection criteria and assessment methods. It is increasingly recognized that it is unrealistic to expect employers to carry out validation studies which are more appropriate to the laboratory than to the realities of the workplace. As an alternative or supplement to the kinds of investigation that *are* possible, the role of systematic JTR analysis is likely to increase, and especially those techniques which specifically recommend appropriate selection criteria and devices. The PAQ is capable of analysing jobs into underlying components or dimensions and, on the basis of known correlations (relationships between different jobs and measures of job performance) a selection test battery or other criteria with intrinsic or synthetic validity can be assembled. In such cases, it may not be necessary to evaluate and justify the selection procedure by conventional models of validation.

(6) Employment legislation

The Equal Pay Act has called into question the justification of established job evaluation systems which can be challenged on the grounds of unfairness (usually to women) because of the intrinsic or institutional biases incorporated. In addition, the increasingly influential Equal Opportunities Commission and the Commission for Racial Equality codes of practice require that employers use selection criteria which are objective, job-related and consistently applied. The techniques of job, task and role analysis are, of course, ideally suited to meeting this need.

References

SPECIFIC METHODS

ANNETT, J., DUNCAN, K.D., STAMMERS, R.B. and GRAY, M.J., *Task Analysis*, Training Information Paper No. 6, London, HMSO, 1971.

BANKS, M.H., JACKSON, P.R., STAFFORD, E.M. and WARR, P.B., *Job Components Inventory Mark II*, Sheffield, Manpower Services Commission, 1979.

DUNCAN, K.D. and KELLY, C.J., *Task Analysis, Learning and the Nature of Transfer*, Sheffield, Manpower Services Commission, 1983.

FINE, S.A. and WILEY, W., *An Introduction to Functional Job Analysis: Methods for Manpower Analysis*, Kalamazoo, Michigan, Upjohn Institute for Employment Research, 1971.

FLANAGAN, J.C., "The Critical Incident Technique", *Psychological Bulletin*, 51 (1954), 327-58.

FLEISHMAN, E.A., "Toward a Taxonomy of Human Performance", *American Psychologist*, 30 (1975), 1127-49
GAEL, S., *Job Analysis: A Guide to Assessing Work Activities*, London, Jossey-Bass, 1983.

LEVINE, E.L., *Everything you always wanted to know about Job Analysis*, Tampa, Florida, Mariner, 1983.

McCORMICK, E.J., JEANNERET, P.R. and MECHAM, R.C., "A Study of Job Characteristics and Job Dimensions as based on the Position Analysis Questionnaire (PAQ)", *Journal of Applied Psychology*, 56 (1972), 347-68.

MANPOWER SERVICES COMMISSION, *Trainer Task Inventory*, Sheffield, Manpower Services Commission, 1984.

PAQ SERVICES INC., "Position Analysis Questionnaire (PAQ)", *Job Analysis Manual*, Logan, Utah, PAQ Services Inc., 1977.

131

PEARN, M.A. and KANDOLA, R.S., *Job-Learning Analysis*, Oxford, Pearn Kandola Downs, 1987.

PRIMOFF, E.S., *How to Prepare and Conduct Job-Element Examinations*, Washington, DC, Office of Personnel and Management, 1974.

RACKHAM, N. and MORGAN, T., *Behaviour Analysis in Training*, London, McGraw-Hill, 1977.

STEWART, V. and STEWART, A., *Business Applications of Repertory Grid*, London, McGraw-Hill, 1981.

GENERAL REFERENCES

BEMIS, S.E., BELENKY, A.H., and SODER, D.A., *Job Analysis: An Effective Management Tool*, Washington, DC, Bureau of National Affairs, 1983.

FLANAGAN, J.C., *Measuring Human Performance*, Pittsburgh, Pennsylvania, American Institute for Research, 1962.

LANDY, F.J., and FARR, J.L., *The Measurement of Work Performance: Methods, Theory and Applications*, Academic Press, London, 1983.

McCORMICK, E.J., "Job and Task Analysis", in M.V. Dunnette (ed.), *Handbook of Industrial and Organisational Psychology*, Chicago, Rand McNally, 1976.

McCORMICK, E.J., *Job Analysis: Methods and Applications*, New York, AMACOM, 1979.

MEISTER, D., *Behavioural Analysis and Measurement Methods*, New York, Wiley, 1985.

PATRICK, J., "Job Analysis, Training and Transferability: Some Theoretical and Practical Issues", in K.D. Duncan, M.M. Gruneberg and D. Wallis, *Changes in Working Life*, Chichester, Wiley, 1980.

ROFF, H.E. and WATSON, T.E., *Job Analysis*, London, Institute of Personnel Management, 1961.

YOUNGMAN, M., OXTOBY, R., MONK, J.D. and HEYWOOD, J., *Analysing Jobs*, Farnborough, Gower, 1978.

Index

135